the best natural
homemade
soaps

the best natural homemade soaps

40 recipes for moisturizing olive oil-based soaps

Mar Gómez

The Best Natural Homemade Soaps
Published originally in Spanish under the title *Jabones Naturales Para Hacer en Casa*
(*Natural Soaps to Make at Home*) © 2009, Editorial Océano, S.L., Barcelona, Spain
Text copyright © 2009, 2014 Mar Gómez
Cover and text design copyright © 2014 Robert Rose Inc.

For complete cataloguing information, see page 216.

Disclaimer

The author and the publisher are not responsible for any adverse effects or consequences resulting
from the use of the information in this book. It is the responsibility of the reader to consult a physician
or other qualified health-care professional regarding his or her personal care.

To the best of our knowledge, the recipes in this book are safe for ordinary use and users. For
those people with allergies or health issues, please read the suggested contents of each recipe carefully
and determine whether or not they may create a problem for you. All recipes are used at the risk of
the consumer.

We cannot be responsible for any hazards, loss or damage that may occur as a result of any
recipe use.

For those with special needs, allergies, requirements or health problems, in the event of
any doubt, please contact your medical adviser prior to the use of any recipe.

Design and production: Daniella Zanchetta/PageWave Graphics Inc.
Editor: Tina Anson Mine
Copy editor/proofreader: Austen Gilliland
Indexer: Beth Zabloski
Translator: Foreign Translations

Cover image: Homemade soap bars © iStockphoto.com/Ivenks
Interior soap photography: Becky Lawton, Océano Ámbar archives
Additional images: p.13 Stacked soap with marigold flower © iStockphoto.com/s-a-m; p.14 Soapwort
plant © iStockphoto.com/membio; p.23 Silicone molds © iStockphoto.com/slkoceva; p.31 Essential oil
with pink flowers © iStockphoto.com/Elena Gaak; p.32 Lavender flowers and oil © iStockphoto.com/
viki2win; p.35 Honey and honeycomb © iStockphoto.com/bereta; p.36 Bowl of clay © iStockphoto.com/
nanka-stalker; p.38 Dried rosebuds © iStockphoto.com/e-belyukova; p.39 Lavender field
© iStockphoto.com/vaide; p.40 Sudsy soap © iStockphoto.com/Rebecca Picard; p.45 Stacked soap
with herbs © iStockphoto.com/s-a-m.

The publisher gratefully acknowledges the financial support of our publishing program by the
Government of Canada through the Canada Book Fund.

Published by Robert Rose Inc.   *OCLC   12/2/14*
120 Eglinton Avenue East, Suite 800
Toronto, Ontario, Canada M4P 1E2
Tel: (416) 322-6552 Fax: (416) 322-6936
www.robertrose.ca

Printed and bound in Canada

1 2 3 4 5 6 7 8 9 TCP 22 21 20 19 18 17 16 15 14

To my girls, Miranda and Alba.
To my family and friends, with all my love.

To Jaco, for his invaluable help,
with all my love.

Contents

Olive oil is one of the most prized Mediterranean products, and the one with the most known virtues. Women in ancient Greece used it to make their hair shine.

History

The first people to manufacture something similar to olive oil soap were the Syrians, in the city of Aleppo. Several thousand years ago, merchants and craftsmen were already producing their famous soap, made with olive oil and bay leaves.

The climate in Syria is quite diverse. The vast majority of the country is a desert, which encourages dry skin and facilitates infections. However, thick Mediterranean forests grow in the mountains of the north, where Aleppo is located, and in the western part of the country. This is where the famous Aleppo pine flourishes.

Near Aleppo, two valuable natural products could easily be obtained: olive oil and bay leaves. They both have great culinary applications, but are also used in cosmetics and natural medicines for their antioxidant and regenerative powers. The women of Aleppo realized that by adding ground bay leaves to soap, skin infections were reduced considerably; the leaves from the bay plant possess an extraordinary natural antiseptic.

Today, Aleppo is one of Syria's principal cities. Its fame is, at least in part, due to this wonderful soap, which has been produced in the region for centuries.

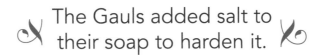

The Gauls added salt to their soap to harden it.

Olive oil soap wasn't the first soap, of course. A mixture of boiled fat and ashes—the main ingredients of soap in ancient times—was first encountered in Babylonia 5,000 years ago. However, in ancient Egypt, people used oil to clean their hair, and preferred spraying themselves with perfume to bathing. The Bible also mentions the use of ashes and oil to clean hair, and the

Ashes

The first soaps were made in the Sumerian era by boiling ashes of different plants in water. The resulting liquid was also used to wash dirty clothes.

Soap in China

In ancient China, bathing rituals were important, and personal cleanliness was taken seriously. But soap as we know it was not widely used in the country until modern times. Detergent-like mixtures made from herbs and vegetables were made, but herbal baths and creams were more commonly used for skin care.

Phoenicians used a similar mixture to clean fabrics. The ancient Greeks used oil for cleaning themselves, which was removed with a kind of scraper that lifted off the dirt along with the oil. Their civilization probably developed the mixture of ashes and animal fat used to produce cakes of soap; however, the Romans took credit for the discovery.

In the 1st century A.D., the Roman historian and naturalist Pliny mentioned the soft soaps used by the Germans and the hard soaps (made with table salt) used by the Gauls. The ruins of a soap factory have been discovered in Pompeii. The soaps made there sometimes contained coloring: they were the so-called *rutilandis capillis* and served to dye hair brilliant colors.

Legend has it that some Roman washerwomen accidentally stumbled upon the creation of soap when plant ashes and animal fat were mixed in the same river. Until then, clothes had been washed according to a method known as "maiden's feet," in which women trod on the clothes in the river's current, allowing the water to wash away the dirt.

 Suds are a modern-day creation in soaps.

With the fall of the Roman Empire, soap fell into disuse, but in the 7th century, in the city of Savona, the Italians begin to make soap again using ashes and fat. The Spanish followed suit, developing their famous Castile soap, which substitutes olive oil for animal fat.

In the 8th century, the Spanish and Italians alike began to make modern soap by mixing animal fat, especially goat fat, with ashes. Beech ashes were the most highly valued due to their fineness. In reality, soap could be made using many different types of ashes and the tallow of whatever animals had

Soapwort

been close at hand. Aromatic plants or flowers, such as rose petals, were added during the preparation of the soap in order to disguise the unpleasant odor of the animal fat. These soaps were used for cleaning.

Until the 12th century, the best soaps were made in southern Europe, especially in Italy and Spain, where it was easy to procure olive oil. Elsewhere in Europe, people commonly used animal fat—even fish fat—and the soaps were of lesser quality. By the 13th century, the French began producing the most coveted soaps, thanks to the addition of olive oil; these soaps were made in the area surrounding Marseille.

 ## Soapwort is a plant that produces a natural soap-like substance.

The Black Death epidemic of the 14th century forced the closure of many public baths, which were common across Europe, because they were believed to be sources of contagion. Washing with soap fell into disuse, including among the nobility, who preferred to drench their bodies in perfume to mask foul odors.

In the early 16th century, soap making caught on again; this time, using olive oil and lye. The English were so enthused about making and using soap that the first American colonists took large quantities of it with them on their initial voyages. They became so accustomed to using it that, when the colonies separated from England centuries later, the settlers began to make their own soap. They made it once a year, using leftover cooking lard—saved specifically for that purpose—and ashes.

Soapwort and Soapbark

Soapwort (*Saponaria officinalis*) is a member of the family Caryophyllaceae, which also includes carnations and pinks. It is native to Europe, but colonists brought the plant to North America when they settled there; it has long since naturalized along roads and riverbanks and is now a considered a common weed in many areas. Its stems and roots contain a sap that, when mixed with water, produces a mildly sudsy lather. A similar substance is found in the inner bark of the Chilean soapbark tree (*Quillaja saponaria*). Extracts of both are components of commercial cleaning and bathing products.

Bacon's Guide to Bathing

English philosopher Sir Francis Bacon (1561–1626) laid out his rules for bathing (sans soap) in his writings on health and medicine. This is the ritual he prescribed: "First before bathing, rub the body and anoint it with oil mixed with some thickening substance, that the power and moistening heat of the bath, rather than the watery part, may enter the body. Next, get into the bath and remain there about two hours. After the bath cover the body with a plaster of mastich, myrrh, gum-dragon, diapalma, and saffron, to keep in the perspiration as much as possible, till the soft matter has by degrees become solid, and keep it on for twenty-four hours or more. Lastly, after taking off the plaster, anoint the body with a mixture of oil, saffron, and salt. Renew the bath with the plaster and unction as before every fifth day, and let the process of softening the body continue for a month."

Spain's Castile soap, made with olive oil from the Mediterranean region, became popular again during the 17th century, and was exported in large quantities. However, it didn't take long for it to be supplanted by Marseille soap, which has the same olive oil–based formula; the French soap became very popular all over Europe and its name is well-known to this day.

In the 18th century, during the reign of Marie Antoinette, Aleppo soap was fashionable, and so was using ashes to wash clothes. The method was simple: clothes were placed in a container, a cloth was placed over them, ashes that had been saved or purchased for this purpose were placed upon the cloth, and hot water was poured through the ashes. This mixture was reheated and re-poured over the clothes several times, then the clothes were left submerged in the mixture until the next day.

This method of washing clothes became so popular that large quantities of ashes were exported, causing the deforestation of major swaths of the Mediterranean. Some historians consider this period largely responsible for the lack of trees in Los Monegros county, in the Aragon region of Spain. During the French Revolution, overzealous logging in France was stopped. As a result, the trees in Los Monegros, in French-occupied Spain, were harvested and burned to create ashes for use as laundry detergent in France. This logging in Spain wouldn't end until after the revolt against Napoleon's troops in the early 1800s.

Soapnuts

Soapnut, or soapberry, trees (*Sapindus* spp.) are relatives of the lychee tree and grow around the world. The trees produce small round fruits that are rich in saponins. When mixed with water, they produce a natural soap substitute that is chemical-free and biodegradable. They've been used for thousands of years by many different populations and are often associated with India—the Latin name of the genus, *Sapindus*, means "soap of India." They are a popular ingredient in Ayurvedic soaps and shampoos.

In 1789, French chemist Nicolas Leblanc made a major breakthrough: He discovered the process for obtaining sodium carbonate, or washing soda, which would revolutionize soap making. In 1791, Leblanc went bankrupt setting up a factory to produce this compound. But that didn't stop sodium carbonate from soon replacing the potassium carbonate (made by washing ashes) that was traditionally used for soap making.

Bracketing the time of Leblanc's discovery, two other major breakthroughs in soap making had occurred. In 1779, Swedish chemist Karl Wilhelm Scheele accidentally discovered a sweet substance we know today as glycerin by boiling olive oil with lead monoxide. Then, in 1823, the Frenchman Michel Eugene Chevreul discovered that glycerin was one of the products of saponification (soap formation), created by the marriage of a fat, such as animal fat or oil, and an alkali, such as sodium carbonate or sodium hydroxide (lye). When the two are combined, the fat breaks down into fatty acids (the soap itself) and glycerin. While the latter is not actually soap, it is often stirred back into the mixture because is a good softening agent and attracts moisture to the skin.

 ## Making soap at home is easy and economical.

When soap began to be produced industrially, it was prepared in large vats using a process called "full cooking," in which fat and lye were cooked until saponification occurred. Then glycerin was extracted, and sold separately. A different industrial process involved neutralizing the resulting fatty acid with sodium carbonate, which allowed the glycerin to be incorporated and its skin-softening benefits to be enjoyed. Over time, several increasingly efficient industrial soap-making methods were developed; they are similar to the ones you will use to make the olive oil soaps in this book.

The tradition of making artisanal soap has continued in rural areas of every country. Some people have dedicated their lives to selling these products, which are increasingly in demand due to their higher quality. The only limit to their creativity is their imagination.

It's time we returned to making our own soap, like our ancestors did. Globalization means we have access to plants and essences from all over the world, and we should take advantage of the possibilities offered by this bounty. All those substances can help you care for your skin. So learn, practice, and then experiment. Personalize your soaps with different shapes and scents, and develop your own soap-making style.

Preparation

Don't worry, we're not going to use large cauldrons, nor are we going to make a whole year's worth of soap in a single day like the pioneers did. We aren't going to save leftover bacon fat, boil it in water, let it cool until it solidifies, clean it of impurities and then mix it with water and lye in a stockpot, stirring and simmering it. Once this mixture cooled, it would produce a simple, practical soap without any traces of the original fat, which isn't bad, but soaps made this way lack character.

The soaps in this book will have plenty of character, and you can prepare them without having to go out into the garden on a windy day or take shelter in a corral. I think it is best to start the process by making a list of utensils, learning how to select the ingredients and getting some guidance on the steps involved in modern soap making.

Taxes

Until the 19th century, soap was considered a luxury item. Governments placed very high taxes on it, and very few people could afford to buy it. For this reason, most of the population had to make it themselves at home.

Utensils

Scale

When making soap, proper measurements are vitally important—it is a form of chemistry, after all. For these recipes, most of the ingredients are measured by weight, not volume, for accuracy. A scale is essential in order to weigh the right proportions of ingredients.

Scales come in a variety of styles. Forget those dial scales with needles that weigh in 1-oz (or 25 gram) increments. If you use one, you'll learn from experience that they aren't nearly accurate enough for these recipes. I advise you to buy a digital scale that weighs up to 11 lbs (5 kg) total, in 0.1-oz (or 1 g) increments. If you're using imperial measurements instead of metric, a scale that reads in increments of 0.01 oz is much better suited to these recipes, which sometimes require very tiny amounts of ingredients, especially in the case of aromatic products.

Precision is important, so choose a scale that is accurate to within 0.1 oz (or 1 g)—or even better, to within 0.01 oz (or 0.5 g). With it, you will be able to precisely weigh the required water, lye and olive oil—not to mention that 0.07 oz (2 g) of lemon essential oil that will give your soap pizzazz.

Look for a scale that has a tare button, as well. This allows you to place a bowl or other receptacle on the scale, then "zero" the scale so that it only weighs the contents. It makes your job so much easier.

Molds

You can use all kinds of molds, as long as they are plastic—although simple coconut shells would do, as well. You can even make the molds yourself, so that the walls can be opened via hinges to extract the block of soap once it has hardened. If you use a rigid plastic mold, bear in mind that it may break when unmolding. It is a good idea to grease the mold with a little oil, or line it with brown paper or plastic wrap so that the soap does not stick to the walls of the mold when you're trying to remove it. A long silicone loaf pan is ideal—look for one with about a 4-cup (1 L) capacity that's 10 to 12 inches (25 to 30 cm) long.

There are all kinds of molds on the market. Check at kitchen stores, hardware stores and even toy stores, where there are molds for modeling clay that can be used to make fun, novel shapes.

Spoons

Choose spoons that are stainless steel, because the lye (also known as caustic soda) will corrode ones made of aluminum or wood. In the latter case, fibers or chemicals used in the wood treatment process can come off the spoon and turn up in the finished soap.

You can grease the mold with a little oil so the finished soap can be easily removed after it has set.

Heat Source

The simplest soap mixtures heat themselves when the lye is mixed with the water. But you will have to heat the olive oil (sometimes mixed with beeswax) separately. To avoid problems and ensure good ventilation, use a portable burner or camping stove that can be moved to a workshop, porch or garden.

Silicone molds

Thermometer

This tool must be made of glass and measure from at least 32°F to 212°F
(0°C to 100°C). Avoid thermometers that have wooden or aluminum bases,
which the lye will corrode. The best and most accurate thermometers are
the ones used in laboratories, which have only the central glass tube without
any housing around it. These thermometers are hygienic and easy to clean,
and lye cannot harm them.

Brown or Parchment Paper

These can be placed underneath the soap when it's drying, after it is cut.
Remember that soap must be dried in the open air, inside the house.

Containers

Always use containers, such as saucepans, made of stainless steel or
enameled cast-iron. Be especially sure that they are not aluminum, because
lye attacks and corrodes anything made of aluminum. If you're using a
measuring cup, choose one made of glass.

Gloves

Always wear rubber gloves to protect your hands, especially when you are handling lye. Keep in mind that lye causes what are called "deep burns"—by the time you realize what has happened, this caustic material has eaten through the skin and attacked the tissue underneath. (In contrast, acid substances attack the skin's surface first, making it easy to feel the burn right away.) To protect yourself when making soap, simply wear the same type of gloves you would use to wash the dishes every day. Medical gloves will work as well, but are thinner.

Goggles

Lye is very dangerous when it comes into contact with the eyes, because it quickly attacks the cornea and is difficult to remove. If lye splashes into your eye, flush it with plenty of water for several minutes, then go to the doctor immediately. It is better to wear glasses of any kind to protect your eyes; they can be sunglasses if you have enough light to work in. The best bet is to buy safety goggles, which are available at many different stores. They are made of plastic and you can even get some with prescription lenses.

Location

The place where you make soap should be well ventilated. Try using a corner of your house near a window or, weather permitting, set up your soap-making operations on the porch. It's always nicer when you work outdoors; in this case, you can use a portable stove like the one you take camping.

If you're indoors and don't have a window nearby that can be opened (or if it is winter), use your materials under the kitchen exhaust hood. The small toxic cloud that forms when water reacts (in any way) with lye is a bit irritating. Although it only lasts a few seconds, it is advisable to stay out of its reach.

You shouldn't make soap around small children. They are curious and may touch an ingredient that could harm them.

By following these simple tips, you won't have any problems making soap at home.

Essential Ingredients

There are only three essential ingredients for making olive oil soap: water, lye (caustic soda) and oil. Historically, the difficulty lay in obtaining the lye, which was made from beech or oak ashes. The lye would have been added to animal fat. Some special additives were already available back then; for instance, essential oils, which could be distilled or macerated using aromatic plants; clay; bits of bay leaf, which is the scent that made Aleppo soap famous; grated orange or lemon zest; violet petals; or, in short, anything that could make that soap better than or preferable over others. Here are guidelines for the ingredients you need to make modern olive oil soap.

Water

Depending on its geographical location, water varies in hardness. For our soaps, soft water is ideal; in other words, it should have low levels of mineral salts, especially calcium. This is more difficult to achieve in some places; for example, on the outer edges of the Iberian Peninsula, there is higher mineral content in the water than in the interior.

It is important for the water you use to be as pure as possible. If you use tap water, let it stand for at least 24 hours to allow the chlorine to evaporate. You can also make these soaps with mineral water (which is specified in the ingredient lists) or spring water with a low mineral content.

For soap making, it is advantageous to use water that contains the smallest possible amount of lime and salt. If you use tap water, let it stand for at least 24 hours to allow the chlorine to evaporate.

 Soap ingredients should be as natural as pure spring water.

Lye (Caustic Soda)

In soap making, the function of lye, or sodium hydroxide, is to react with fats to produce fatty acids and glycerin. In these homemade soaps, the glycerin is not removed, so we will be able to exploit of all its natural properties, such as its softening and moisturizing abilities, which are so important for the skin. In ancient times, lye was made by washing wood ashes. Of course, this lye was not pure; it depended on the wood that was used and contained many contaminants.

In contrast to the hard soaps in this book, soft soaps are made with potash, or potassium hydroxide, which, when mixed with fat, produces a

Always use natural products as soap additives. Your skin will thank you for it.

100% Pure
Beeswax

GLYCERIN

more liquid soap. You can use a mix of potash, water and leftover cooking fat to make a soap that effectively fights aphids in the garden and can be used for watering plants. Potash is also used to make the liquid soaps used in shampoos or pump dispensers.

For these recipes, we will limit ourselves to buying lye, also called caustic soda or sodium hydroxide, which is sold in flakes, pellets or granules. Look for it at cleaning or soap-making supply stores. Don't confuse it with lye-based drain cleaners, which contain additives—it should be labeled 100% sodium hydroxide.

Oil

Olive oil is the main ingredient in the homemade soaps discussed in this book. Its good properties are known to just about everyone: it is rich in vitamins, minerals and protein. In the kitchen, it is the oil most beneficial to your health; in cosmetics, it has been used since ancient times because of its virtues for hair and skin. Use the highest quality extra virgin or virgin olive oil you can find to create the best soap.

You can actually use many different oils to make soap; each one gives different results. After olive oil, the highest rated oils for soap making are almond oil, because it soothes irritated skin; marigold oil, because it is antiseptic and aids in the formation of scar tissue; wheat germ and flaxseed oils, because they contain antioxidants; palm oil, because it is soft and gentle; and castor oil, because it has good moisturizing abilities.

You will not have to do these calculations for the soap recipes in this book, but you should know that the necessary amount of oil needed to react completely with 2.2 lbs (1 kg) lye is different for each type of oil. This is called the *saponification value* and it varies a little, from 4.8 oz (136 grams) for olive oil to 6.5 oz (184 g) for coconut oil. Castor, corn, hazelnut, soybean and sunflower oils have values similar to those of olive oil.

Additives

If you observe the composition of commercial soaps, you will see that the number of ingredients increases with the quality of the product. However, we won't be using industrially prepared chemicals—we are interested in a series of natural products that can help to improve the quality of a soap. They might make the soap harder or softer, make it greasier or foamier, or give it greater cleansing capacity; for these effects, we will add beeswax, cocoa butter, kaolin clay, seaweed, goat's milk and so on. However, none of these ingredients is quite as important as the additives that provide the aroma, that hint of a perpetual fresh breeze that we want to get out of a good soap. To do this, we need essential oils.

Essential Oils

It is important to understand the difference between natural essences, artificial essences, mineral oils and essential oils. Let's rule out petroleum-derived mineral oils and artificial, or synthetic, essences. Although they are used in cosmetics and the essences mimic natural aromas, both are products made in laboratories.

The difference between natural essences and essential oils is sometimes a matter of semantics—the terms are often used interchangeably. However, scents sold in the form of essences are usually less concentrated and pure than essential oils, and their

Essential oils are intensely aromatic substances that contain the essence of plant scents. Their high concentration means they should not be applied directly to the skin. They must always be diluted in other carrier oils, or diluted in hot water if the aroma is to be inhaled.

fragrance doesn't last as long. For our purposes, we are going to use essential oils of the highest purity, which we will add to the soap mixture right before it is placed in the mold.

Essential oils may be made from the bark, roots, seeds, resins, flowers, leaves or wood of some trees and shrubs. Each has its own characteristics, depending on which part of the plant is used.

The name of the finished essential oil depends on the part of the plant from which the extraction was made. For instance, several essential oils are extracted from the orange tree. If the oil is from the orange zest, it will

Methods for Obtaining Essential Oils

- **Press.** In ancient Egypt, essential oils were made by pressing plants and letting the resulting liquid sit in the desert under the sand until the water evaporated and only the oil was left. The results were extraordinary. The lotus blossom perfume found in Tutankhamen's tomb reaches us almost intact to this day, even after 3,000 years.

- **Ethanol extraction.** Another method that does not require heat is ethanol extraction, which is preferable to distillation for certain plants, such as boldo *(Peumus boldus)*. In this case, plants are chopped and steeped in ethyl alcohol (ethanol) for several weeks so that the alcohol may be filtered later. This is how the famous Hungary water—made with rosemary, mint, rose petals, lemon zest and orange blossom water—is prepared. All you need is one month in order to prepare this fragrant essence.

- **Maceration.** Cold maceration is accomplished by submerging chopped plants in oil or water for a period of time. Hot maceration is accomplished by heating oil (or fat) before adding the plant. Other forms of maceration are carried out using an inorganic solvent, such as benzene, which is eliminated with alcohol.

- **Distillation.** This process is done by putting water and the chopped plant in a still and bringing the mixture to a boil. The steam produced is cooled in the still's pipe, and the resulting liquid that drips down contains essential oil with some distilled water, called hydrolate. This may be separated via decantation.

be called orange essential oil. If it comes from the leaves and small branches, it is called petitgrain essential oil. If it is extracted from the flowers of the orange tree (orange blossoms), it is a very expensive and fragrant type called neroli essential oil.

Note that some essential oils are harmful to pregnant women: these include basil, cypress, hyssop, marjoram, lemon balm (Melissa), sage and thyme oils. But you can use eucalyptus, lavender, chamomile, peppermint, rosemary and many others. You can make these at home since the plants are easy to find.

 Be careful with essential oils—they are intense, concentrated compounds.

Beeswax

This substance makes soap harder, in addition to adding its inherent protective properties to the mix. It is well known that bees produce this wax in order to make honeycomb. Once it is filtered, beeswax has a plethora of uses for humans. If distilled, it becomes an oil with a variety of therapeutic uses. You can find beeswax sold in bulk, in blocks of different weights or formed into pearls. You can use either; grate large blocks so that they melt more quickly and easily when combined with the warm olive oil. Ideally, beeswax should be minimally processed and as natural as possible. The color of beeswax available on the market ranges from intense yellow to white. White is used for making nourishing creams.

Cocoa Butter

This additive comes from the fat contained in cocoa beans. It is very greasy and easily melts at body temperature. It is used in cosmetics to make creams, lipstick and so forth. It is also used for cooking, in recipes that require its characteristic texture and flavor. Cocoa butter is also a softening agent, like

Bees are extraordinary producers of natural substances, including honey, beeswax and propolis—all of which have known medicinal properties. Honey also gives soap an unexpected softness and aroma.

Clay has been valued since
ancient times for its many
outstanding beauty- and
health-enhancing properties.

alcohol; that is, it serves to create a softer mixture. Look for blocks of pure cocoa butter sold in bulk at specialty shops and pharmacies.

Alcohol

This is sometimes added to soften soap. However, if added in excess, it can adversely affect the fragrance and dry out the skin—not to mention softening the soap too much and making it more difficult to form.

Glycerin and Other Softening Agents

In the recipes in this book, enough glycerin is formed during saponification that it is not required as an additive. However, extra glycerin is sometimes added to soften a soap mixture further and increase its smoothness.

Cocoa butter is the main ingredient in classic lip balms. It prevents skin from drying out, and it doesn't spoil.

Milk

Rich in proteins, minerals and vitamins, milk is a common soap additive. Goat's milk is often used.

Clay

With outstanding health-enhancing properties that are constantly expanding, clay is used as a poultice to treat aching bones, liver inflammation, all types of hair problems, kidney stones, athlete's foot, psoriasis, ulcers and more. It can be applied as a face mask, used for full-body clay baths and ingested by the teaspoon for a few days to strengthen the heart and lower blood pressure. It is always good to have clay soap on hand for a good skin cleansing.

Bran

Bran is the outer husk of a grain kernel. It is added to soaps as an exfoliant, like almond and oat flours.

Honey

Often added as a softening agent, honey lends soap a unique scent.

Flowers and Plants

Be careful when choosing plants for soap making. Avoid picking them in polluted spots or near highways. If you're going to pick them yourself, do it far away from big cities, in uncontaminated areas. Another possibility is to buy plants in packages from a trusted source. The number of plants that can be used as soap additives is enormous: the flowers of mallow, chamomile, lavender, rosemary and roses; spices, such as cinnamon or cloves; and vegetables, such as avocados, cucumbers, carrots and seaweed are just a few wonderful examples.

 It's a good idea to go out into the country in the spring or summer and pick a few bunches of lavender for soap making.

Lavender has one of the most coveted scents in the artisan soap market.

Soap Making Overview

See pages 42–44 for full step-by-step instructions.

Weigh the water and pour it into a large saucepan. (Step 1)

Carefully stir in the lye. (Step 2)

Slowly add the lye mixture to the hot oil. (Step 4)

Now it's time to pour in the additives. (Step 7)

Stir the mixture without making foam. (Step 8)

Pour the mixture into a soap mold. (Step 9)

Cover and let stand for 48 hours. (Step 11)

Empty the mold and wait for another 24 hours. (Step 11)

Cut the soap to the desired size. (Step 12)

Step-by-Step Instructions

Aleppo soap continues to be manufactured as it has been for hundreds of years. When the Syrians started making it, crushed bay leaves were added, but once distillation was discovered, they began making it with the essential oil from this plant. Lye was obtained by burning glasswort plants, which grow in damp ground, for hours underground. The resulting ashes were washed to produce lye; these ashes were highly valued by potters as well. Here's how to prepare olive oil soap with the modern forms of these basic ingredients, using a simple step-by-step process you can follow at home.

1. Protect your hands and eyes with gloves and goggles. Weigh the water (or infusion, juice, milk or other liquid) and the lye separately, in the quantities listed in the recipe. Pour the water (or other liquid) into a large saucepan.

2. Slowly stir the lye into the water (or other liquid). Stir gently until the lye is dissolved. The temperature of the mixture will rise; monitor it with a thermometer until the mixture is between 120°F and 140°F (49°C and 60°C).

CAUTION

Lye is very corrosive; be careful to not touch it with your hands. Once mixed with oil, it softens, though it is still caustic. When you mix lye into water, a puff of irritating vapor will rise, so make sure you are in a well-ventilated area or turn on the kitchen exhaust hood. Never pour water over lye—it can erupt and splatter, causing burns. Always stir lye into water slowly and carefully.

3. Meanwhile, in a separate saucepan, heat the olive oil to between 120°F and 140°F (49°C and 60°C). If the recipe contains beeswax, this is the time to stir it in slowly.

4. Add the lye mixture to the olive oil and stir slowly, trying not to splash. Remember to keep your goggles on, as even a diluted lye splatter can be quite painful.

5. Stir occasionally, every 15 minutes or so, until the mixture thickens and develops a texture similar to that of light mayonnaise. If you need another way to check the consistency, scoop up a bit of the soap mixture with a spoon and drizzle it in a circle over the mixture in the pan. If the circle you "drew" stays on the surface for a few seconds, it means the soap is properly congealed.

6. One way to significantly reduce the time it takes for soap to congeal is to use an immersion blender (also known as a stick blender). Use it carefully, without raising the blender head from the bottom of the pot. You should ideally stir by hand the first time, wait 15 minutes, stir by hand again, then, right after that, stir with the immersion blender for 3 or 4 minutes. Let the mixture stand, then stir again, if necessary.

7. After the soap congeals, it is time to add any essential oils and the rest of the additives—plants, cocoa butter, clay, etc.—to achieve the desired effect. (The exceptions are beeswax, which is added to the heating oil, and goat's milk, which replaces the initial water.) These ingredients are what make one soap different from another and give them their character.

8. Stir the soap mixture for 1 minute with a spoon or a whisk (not the immersion blender), taking care not to create foam, to finish the soapmaking process.

9. Pour the finished soap into a mold that has been greased with a little oil, or lined with brown paper or plastic wrap, to prevent the mixture from sticking. Try out different molds, in the form of animals, shells or whatever pleases you, to create individual designs. You can also place lemon or orange slices on top of the soap, sprinkle it with mint leaves or carve a figure into the bar as it's being shaped.

10. Gently tap the mold so that any air bubbles rise to the surface and disappear, because they will ruin the soap's appearance.

11. Cover the soap with a blanket or towel and let it stand for 2 days. If it is a very large mold, uncover it and let it stand for an additional 1 day. Unmold the soap. Wait for another 24 hours, then cut it into bars or pieces according to your preference. They should not be too small, because they need to be a practical size.

12. Once cut, let the soap dry for 1 month, turning it over every once in a while so that it dries uniformly. Make sure that the place where it is drying in your house is neither too damp nor too warm, and that air circulates freely around the soap. The easiest thing to do is place the bars on brown or tracing paper on top of a cabinet. Whatever you do, do not place the soap inside any piece of furniture.

13. Once the drying time is completed, store the soap in a wooden or cardboard box inside a cabinet.

14. Soap prepared in this fashion will keep for years. Don't panic if it dries out; when you get it wet, it will rehydrate itself.

Yield

Each of these recipes yields 2.2 lbs (1 kg) of soap.
If desired, you can make a double batch or a half-batch
by adjusting the measurements of each ingredient.

Helpful Tips

Natural Is Best

Remember that these soaps have a therapeutic function. In other words, in addition to cleansing, they can help you correct specific problems, generally on the skin. People do not need soaps with bright colors or artificial scents (that's what perfumes are for).

Making Infusions

In some recipes, you'll use an infusion instead of water as the base. Prepare it as you normally would any infusion: heat water to a boil and pour into a bowl that contains the herb or plant you're going to use. Cover it and let it stand for 5 minutes. Strain and weigh the quantity you need for the recipe.

Adding Additional Scent

The amount of essential oil added to each soap recipe is intended as a guideline. You can add a larger amount to the mixture if you so desire. About 1 tbsp (15 mL) essential oil—around 300 drops—per 2.2 lbs (1 kg) of soap is the highest recommended dose. This amount will yield an extremely fragrant soap.

Temperature

The soaps in this book create more lather with hot water than with cold water. The only exception is Clay Soap (page 167), which shouldn't be used with hot water, because it may cause red bumps on the skin. However, when used with cold water, it produces a spectacular effect.

Drain Soap Well

Don't leave homemade soap in a soap dish without a grate in the bottom. The bar will soften up too much, and it will begin to melt away if it stands in water.

Recipes

OLIVE OIL SOAP

The Original Soap

This recipe makes the original Castile soap, just like the one our grandmothers made. It has been prepared for generations in all types of households, and can be enhanced with the essences we like most. This is what soap manufactured in southern Europe was like before lye was produced industrially. Only water, olive oil and fragrances obtained from infusions or macerations made at home with aromatic plants were added to the lye, which was produced in small workshops.

In some cases, people added essential oils, which could be created through distillation using a homemade still—something that was not impossible or too expensive if they gathered the resources and had the urge to do so. In order to set themselves apart, wealthy people bought soaps scented with expensive, imported essential oils such as sandalwood and citronella.

The most common and economical way to add fragrance was to store blocks of prepared soap inside a box to which pieces of orange, lemon or grapefruit zest had been added. Thyme, lavender and rosemary could also be spread over the soap. The wooden or cardboard box was then tightly covered for at least one month. After this time had elapsed, the soap was infused with the scent. This tradition was related to me by a group of octogenarian women in the Extremadura region of Spain.

The world's most ancient oil is probably the one made from the argan, a tree that only grows in southwestern Morocco on slopes that face the sea. It produces a fruit similar to the olive from which an extraordinary oil for the skin is extracted.

Another wonderful oil of similar antiquity is sesame oil, used in Ayurvedic medicine since ancient times. It improves skin texture and gives the skin luster and vitality while it soothes and strengthens.

Olive Oil Soap

Olive oil has been used for thousands of years in the Mediterranean, as food and as a soap ingredient.

Note: Exact measurements are crucial in soap making. Turn to page 21 for how-tos.

7.5 oz	mineral water	213 g
3 oz	lye (caustic soda)	85 g
1.5 lbs	extra virgin olive oil	682 g
	Scent (optional), store-bought or homemade	

1. Wearing gloves and goggles, pour mineral water into a large saucepan. Add lye slowly, stirring gently until it is dissolved.

2. Using a thermometer, monitor the temperature of the lye mixture until it is between 120°F and 140°F (49°C and 60°C).

3. Meanwhile, in a separate saucepan, heat olive oil to between 120°F and 140°F (49°C and 60°C).

4. Remove olive oil from heat. Add lye mixture to olive oil, stirring slowly and trying not to splash.

5. Stir occasionally, every 15 minutes or so, until the mixture thickens and congeals. (It will have a texture similar to that of light mayonnaise.)

6. Stir in scent (if using). Stir for 1 minute with a spoon (or with a whisk, taking care not to create foam).

7. Pour into a greased or paper-lined soap mold. Gently tap mold to remove any air bubbles.

8. Cover with a blanket or towel and let stand for 2 days. Uncover and let stand for an additional day if the mold is very large.

9. Turn soap out of mold. Wait another day, then cut into bars as desired.

10. Dry bars for 1 month, turning occasionally to ensure they are drying uniformly.

Olive Oil Soap's Action on the Skin

- This basic soap, to which fragrance is added as desired, is beneficial for all skin types as long as the users do not suffer from any ailment that requires more specific care, such as eczema.

- If the mixture is not stirred during the saponification process (when the soap is formed in the saucepan), the glycerin created will remain on the bottom of the pan and not mix into the soap. On the other hand, if you were mixing, for instance, coconut oil and lard, you would have to add table salt for the precipitation to be more complete, and then remove the excess lye and glycerin. By making soap in the manner outlined in these recipes, the glycerin remains integrated in the soap. In any case, glycerin has known beneficial effects on skin: it prevents it from drying out too much, helps heal wounds and improves most skin ailments.

- If you don't add any scent, the soap will not leave any perfume behind on the skin.

SEAWEED SOAP

The Most Purifying Soap

You can use any type of seaweed on the market to make this soap. There is a wide variety: karengo, dulse, wakame, nori, kombu, agar-agar, Irish moss (which is the source of carageenan), arame, hijiki and so on.

Any variety of seaweed will do because all are rich in minerals, especially iodine, which are beneficial to the skin. Seaweed purifies the body and alkalinizes the blood when eaten in small amounts. It also has a purifying effect when used on the skin.

You can buy seaweed at specialty and herbalists' shops; some large supermarkets also sell different types in the produce section. Seaweed is sold dried and packaged. If you cook with it, you usually have to rehydrate it in salt water. This is not necessary for these soaps—you can use dried seaweed and break up any large chunks.

The fucus seaweed (*Fucus vesiculosus*) that we will use in this recipe is a brownish seaweed that grows in northern European seas. It is a source of iodine and used as a thyroid stimulant in weight-loss diets. Otherwise, fucus has the same properties as other seaweeds. It does have one peculiarity: when ingested, or used in creams and extracts, it helps reduce fluid retention and fat deposits.

Marjoram essential oil gives this soap its sweet and penetrating aroma, which is reminiscent of mint.

Seaweed Soap

This soap absorbs impurities, hydrates thirsty skin, removes lipids and fights cellulite.

Tips

Seaweed purifies the body. Therefore, if it is used externally, it will also have a purifying effect on the skin.

To make the fucus seaweed infusion, in a bowl, pour 7.5 oz (213 g) boiling water over 1 tbsp (15 mL) dried fucus seaweed. Cover and let stand for 5 minutes. Strain and weigh for recipe.

Fun Facts

Seaweed is about two billion years old.

Seaweed is taken when the body is in a weakened state in order to recover health. Applied externally, it is excellent for rehydrating and firming skin cells.

Note: Exact measurements are crucial in soap making. Turn to page 21 for how-tos.

7.5 oz	fucus seaweed infusion (see tips, at left)	213 g
3 oz	lye (caustic soda)	85 g
1.5 lbs	extra virgin olive oil	682 g
1 tbsp	dried fucus seaweed	15 mL
0.18 oz	marjoram essential oil	5 g

1. Wearing gloves and goggles, pour fucus infusion into a large saucepan. Add lye slowly, stirring gently until it is dissolved.

2. Using a thermometer, monitor the temperature of the lye mixture until it is between 120°F and 140°F (49°C and 60°C).

3. Meanwhile, in a separate saucepan, heat olive oil to between 120°F and 140°F (49°C and 60°C).

4. Remove olive oil from heat. Add lye mixture to olive oil, stirring slowly and trying not to splash.

5. Stir occasionally, every 15 minutes or so, until the mixture thickens and congeals. (It will have a texture similar to that of light mayonnaise.)

6. Stir in dried seaweed and essential oil. Stir for 1 minute with a spoon (or with a whisk, taking care not to create any foam).

7. Pour into a greased or paper-lined soap mold. Gently tap mold to remove any air bubbles.

8. Cover with a blanket or towel and let stand for 2 days. Uncover and let stand for an additional day if the mold is very large.

9. Turn soap out of mold. Wait another day, then cut into bars as desired.

10. Dry bars for 1 month, turning occasionally to ensure they are drying uniformly.

Seaweed Soap's Action on the Skin

- This soap is primarily purifying and remineralizing.

- It is ideal for weak skin that has impurities.

- Soap made with fucus seaweed fights cellulite. Apply it directly to areas where fat has accumulated, rubbing the bar in circles over the affected parts.

POLLEN SOAP

The Bread of Bees

Pollen is the masculine essence that fertilizes a plant's ovum. The pollen sold in stores is a mix of many different pollens from a wide variety of flowers. Bees mix tiny particles of plant pollen with secretions that they produce in order to create the small granules that you find in packages at the grocery store.

Pollen soap is one of my favorites, and it is a soap that gives the best results when used regularly. Its best characteristic is the beneficial action it has on acne-prone skin, thanks to its concentration of carotene, which the body transforms into vitamin A. Pollen also contains vitamins B, C, D, E and K, as well as minerals and amino acids.

The applications for pollen in cosmetics are exceptional, thanks to its rich composition. In addition to being beneficial for acne, it is also a potent revitalizer, making it equally helpful for undernourished and wrinkled skin.

When buying pollen, consider several factors: it should be fresh (when pollen is more than a year old, it loses almost 80% of its helpful properties) and its expiration date should not be coming up soon. In addition, it should be various colors, including yellow, orange, purple and black. Fresh pollen dissolves easily in your mouth or in plain water.

There are two ways to add pollen to soap: in its original, granulated form or ground (using a clean coffee grinder).

Pollen Soap

7.5 oz	mineral water	213 g
3 oz	lye (caustic soda)	85 g
1.5 lbs	extra virgin olive oil	682 g
0.35 oz	beeswax	10 g
1 tbsp	granulated pollen	15 mL
15	drops mint essential oil	15

1. Wearing gloves and goggles, pour mineral water into a large saucepan. Add lye slowly, stirring gently until it is dissolved.

2. Using a thermometer, monitor the temperature of the lye mixture until it is between 120°F and 140°F (49°C and 60°C).

3. Meanwhile, in a separate saucepan, heat olive oil to between 120°F and 140°F (49°C and 60°C), stirring in beeswax slowly.

4. Remove olive oil mixture from heat. Add lye mixture to olive oil mixture, stirring slowly and trying not to splash.

5. Stir occasionally, every 15 minutes or so, until the mixture thickens and congeals. (It will have a texture similar to that of light mayonnaise.)

6. Stir in pollen and essential oil. Stir for 1 minute with a spoon (or with a whisk, taking care not to create foam).

7. Pour into a greased or paper-lined soap mold. Gently tap mold to remove any air bubbles.

8. Cover with a blanket or towel and let stand for 2 days. Uncover and let stand for an additional day if the mold is very large.

9. Turn soap out of mold. Wait another day, then cut into bars as desired.

10. Dry bars for 1 month, turning occasionally to ensure they are drying uniformly.

Pollen Soap's Action on the Skin

❧ Pollen soap is indicated for everyone who has problems with acne or oily skin, for skin with large pores and blackheads, and for mature skin with premature wrinkles.

❧ The biggest virtue of pollen soap is that it nourishes skin.

❧ I do not recommend this soap for people who are allergic to pollen.

SANDALWOOD SOAP

The Aroma of the Sacred Tree

Sandalwood (*Santalum album*) belongs to the Santalaceae family. Sandalwood essential oil is obtained from the wood and roots of the tree, which originated in the Far East. In India, where the best specimens grow, sandalwood trees are considered sacred and can only be felled when they are more than 30 years old, because this species grows very slowly.

The wood is used mainly in cabinetmaking, and the resulting shavings are used to create essential oils, which are said to help people attain spiritual harmony.

This scent has many applications, for both internal and external disorders. Its aroma is powerful and intense, and it is used extensively in cosmetics, perfumes, incense and soap. Because sandalwood has a very masculine scent, many fragrances for men include it in their composition.

For this soap, you will use sandalwood chips to make the infusion and sandalwood essential oil as an extra additive.

Sandalwood Soap

Indian sandalwood evokes a world of mystery, sanctity and devotion. Its virtue lies in its essential aroma. It also fights acne and heals dehydrated and damaged skin.

Tip

To make the sandalwood infusion, in a bowl, pour 7.5 oz (213 g) boiling water over 1 tbsp (15 mL) sandalwood chips. Cover and let stand for 5 minutes. Strain and weigh for recipe.

• • •

Fun Fact

Sandalwood powerfully stimulates the sensation of divinity. For that reason, the Egyptians burned it in their temples, and Hindus have been doing the same since time immemorial.

Note: Exact measurements are crucial in soap making. Turn to page 21 for how-tos.

7.5 oz	sandalwood infusion (see tip, at left)	213 g
3 oz	lye (caustic soda)	85 g
1.5 lbs	extra virgin olive oil	682 g
0.35 oz	sandalwood essential oil	10 g

1. Wearing gloves and goggles, pour sandalwood infusion into a large saucepan. Add lye slowly, stirring gently until it is dissolved.

2. Using a thermometer, monitor the temperature of the lye mixture until it is between 120°F and 140°F (49°C and 60°C).

3. Meanwhile, in a separate saucepan, heat olive oil to between 120°F and 140°F (49°C and 60°C).

4. Remove olive oil from heat. Add lye mixture to olive oil, stirring slowly and trying not to splash.

5. Stir occasionally, every 15 minutes or so, until the mixture thickens and congeals. (It will have a texture similar to that of light mayonnaise.)

6. Stir in essential oil. Stir for 1 minute with a spoon (or with a whisk, taking care not to create foam).

7. Pour into a greased or paper-lined soap mold. Gently tap mold to remove any air bubbles.

8. Cover with a blanket or towel and let stand for 2 days. Uncover and let stand for an additional day if the mold is very large.

9. Turn soap out of mold. Wait another day, then cut into bars as desired.

10. Dry bars for 1 month, turning occasionally to ensure they are drying uniformly.

Sandalwood Soap's Action on the Skin

❧ As with all of the soaps in this book, this one is good for the face and the body.

❧ Sandalwood is exceptional for the skin because it not only fights acne and oily skin but also soothes dehydrated and damaged skin. It produces very good results on men's skin when used after shaving. It is a disinfectant and combats infections caused by rebellious ingrown hairs and other problems caused by daily shaving.

❧ Many plants and essential oils do not have just one therapeutic property but several, which can seem contradictory. We often come across cases like this one, where the same compound is beneficial in opposite cases, such as excess oiliness and dryness.

KIWI SOAP

The Scent of the South Seas

The kiwifruit (*Actinidia deliciosa*) is very high in vitamins, especially vitamin C, and contains a large amount of fiber. Therefore, this soap stimulates the skin's defense mechanisms and prevents infections of all kinds. It is beneficial for skin of all ages.

When preparing the soap, we'll use a whole kiwifruit, mashed with a fork. If you use it this way, you exploit all of its healthful properties. The kiwi should, ideally, be ripe.

If you like, you can add the kiwi's skin to the soap. Note, however, that most commercial fruits are sprayed, and pesticides and fungicides are deposited on the skin. If you add the kiwi skin to the soap, you will be adding this group of harmful substances. Avoiding this problem is as simple as buying organically grown kiwis. This type of agriculture does not use toxic substances to treat pests. If you do add the skin, chop it finely, or use it as desired to decorate the top of the soap.

You can use any variety of kiwifruit, whether it has green pulp or yellow pulp. Yellow is relatively new to the markets.

Kiwi Soap

Fun Fact

The kiwifruit is native to China and was introduced to New Zealand in the 1950s. There, it was given the name kiwi, the same moniker as the national bird, which is named for its song.

Note: Exact measurements are crucial in soap making. Turn to page 21 for how-tos.

7.5 oz	mineral water	213 g
3 oz	lye (caustic soda)	85 g
1.5 lbs	extra virgin olive oil	682 g
1	kiwifruit, peeled and mashed (skin chopped finely, optional)	1
0.1 oz	lemon essential oil	3 g

1. Wearing gloves and goggles, pour mineral water into a large saucepan. Add lye slowly, stirring gently until it is dissolved.

2. Using a thermometer, monitor the temperature of the lye mixture until it is between 120°F and 140°F (49°C and 60°C).

3. Meanwhile, in a separate saucepan, heat olive oil to between 120°F and 140°F (49°C and 60°C).

4. Remove olive oil from heat. Add lye mixture to olive oil, stirring slowly and trying not to splash.

5. Stir occasionally, every 15 minutes or so, until the mixture thickens and congeals. (It will have a texture similar to that of light mayonnaise.)

6. Stir in mashed kiwi, kiwi skin (if using) and essential oil. Stir for 1 minute with a spoon (or with a whisk, taking care not to create foam).

7. Pour into a greased or paper-lined soap mold. Gently tap mold to remove any air bubbles.

8. Cover with a blanket or towel and let stand for 2 days. Uncover and let stand for an additional day if the mold is very large.

9. Turn soap out of mold. Wait another day, then cut into bars as desired.

10. Dry bars for 1 month, turning occasionally to ensure they are drying uniformly.

Kiwi Soap's Action on the Skin

- This soap is recommended for all skin types, especially in the summer, when skin is exposed to many types of bacteria in swimming pools and on beaches.

- Like all other soaps, it can be used on the face and body.

- If you add the kiwi skin, the soap will have a slight exfoliating effect. Massage the soap directly on the skin in order to experience this benefit.

- Kiwi soap yields very good results for people with sensitive skin.

CARROT SOAP

The Essence of the Earth

The carrot (*Daucus carota*) is very rich in vitamin A and is essential for maintaining healthy skin.

For this soap, finely grate the carrot or finely chop it in a food processor. It is preferable to use fresh young carrots. If you use carrots that are very thick or old, they will be tough and fibrous, and the resulting soap will not have the same healing qualities or pleasing appearance (although the latter aspect is less important).

Carrot essential oil must be of the wild variety: this oil is obtained by distilling carrot seeds. Its aroma soothes the mind, and the oil is antimicrobial. While its Latin name, *Daucus carota*, is the same as that of the edible garden carrot, the wild variety is found only in uncultivated fields in Central Asia and the United States.

This soap offers many advantages to people who have mature skin or who have skin with many wrinkles, even if they are young. It can be used by people who are prone to rashes caused by allergies brought on by exposure to synthetic materials used in textiles.

It's smart to be sun-safe, but if you choose to get a bit of color in the summertime, this soap will help maintain your suntan for a longer period of time.

Carrot Soap

This soap is ideal for mature or leathery skin creased by wrinkles caused by the sun and the elements.

Tip

Carrot soap is only slightly aromatic; to give it a different character, add some neroli essential oil, which is made from bitter oranges and used in aromatherapy as an antidepressant.

• • •

Fun Fact

When ingested, beta carotene (a form of vitamin A), stimulates the production of melanin, your best ally against the sun. Vitamin A should be present both in your diet and your cosmetics.

Note: Exact measurements are crucial in soap making. Turn to page 21 for how-tos.

7.5 oz	mineral water	213 g
3 oz	lye (caustic soda)	85 g
1.5 lbs	extra virgin olive oil	682 g
1	carrot, finely grated or chopped	1
	Juice of half a lemon	
0.15 oz	carrot essential oil	4 g

1. Wearing gloves and goggles, pour mineral water into a large saucepan. Add lye slowly, stirring gently until it is dissolved.

2. Using a thermometer, monitor the temperature of the lye mixture until it is between 120°F and 140°F (49°C and 60°C).

3. Meanwhile, in a separate saucepan, heat olive oil to between 120°F and 140°F (49°C and 60°C).

4. Remove olive oil from heat. Add lye mixture to olive oil, stirring slowly and trying not to splash.

5. Stir occasionally, every 15 minutes or so, until the mixture thickens and congeals. (It will have a texture similar to that of light mayonnaise.)

6. Stir in carrot, lemon juice and essential oil. Stir for 1 minute with a spoon (or with a whisk, taking care not to create foam).

7. Pour into a greased or paper-lined soap mold. Gently tap mold to remove any air bubbles.

8. Cover with a blanket or towel and let stand for 2 days. Uncover and let stand for an additional day if the mold is very large.

9. Turn soap out of mold. Wait another day, then cut into bars as desired.

10. Dry bars for 1 month, turning occasionally to ensure they are drying uniformly.

Carrot Soap's Action on the Skin

- Because of its high vitamin A content, this soap is very beneficial in treating dermatitis, eczema and psoriasis, and rejuvenating mature and wrinkled skin.

- The soap's action is enhanced by vitamin C, which is present in the added lemon juice. Carrot essential oil also contains a number of different natural compounds that add very subtle layers of fragrance: limonene and dipentene (lemon), geraniol (rose or geranium) and beta-caryophyllene (clove).

- Young skin that has not been properly cared for often exhibits signs of premature aging. To prevent this problem, your diet and/or cosmetics should contain vitamin A, which stimulates the production of melanin, and vitamin C, an antioxidant.

LEMON SOAP

The Perfect Stimulant

The lemon (*Citrus limon*) is a small tree native to Asia that belongs to the Rutaceae family—the same one as the orange—but it tolerates the cold better. Its fruit is called the lemon, too.

It is well known that the lemon, like all citrus fruits, is rich in vitamin C. Traditionally, it is considered a cure-all—and there is good reason to think this. Its juice is used as a purgative (laxative) and as a depurative (a compound that frees the body of impurities), and is taken to treat canker sores, chilblains, warts and more.

Numerous ailments are treated with lemon essential oil, such as boils, herpes and excessively oily skin. When using it, keep in mind that it is phototoxic; in other words, if you apply this oil and expose yourself to the sun, your skin can develop spots.

For this soap, we will use freshly squeezed lemon juice and essential oil made from lemons or limes (*Citrus aurantifolia*), a close relative of the lemon.

If you like, you can add lemon zest to the soap, grated to the thickness of your choice. You can even cut it with a knife into small strips and add it at the end to improve the soap's appearance. As in other cases in which fruit skin is added, choose organically grown fruits in order to avoid including unwanted substances in your soap.

Lemon essential oil is used in many creams, tonics, soaps and cosmetics. It is also widely used in food, for flavoring everything from beverages to desserts.

Lemon Soap

This soap has a very positive effect on oily skin but also regulates combination skin.

Tip

Lemon soap accepts many other natural additives, such as thyme, which adds an incredible aromatic surprise. Thyme strengthens nails and eliminates skin spots, too.

Note: Exact measurements are crucial in soap making. Turn to page 21 for how-tos.

4 oz	mineral water	113 g
3.5 oz	lemon juice	100 g
3 oz	lye (caustic soda)	85 g
1.5 lbs	extra virgin olive oil	682 g
0.35 oz	beeswax	10 g
	Grated zest of 1 large lemon	
0.18 oz	lemon essential oil	5 g

1. Wearing gloves and goggles, pour mineral water and lemon juice into a large saucepan. Add lye slowly, stirring gently until it is dissolved.

2. Using a thermometer, monitor the temperature of the lye mixture until it is between 120°F and 140°F (49°C and 60°C).

3. Meanwhile, in a separate saucepan, heat olive oil to between 120°F and 140°F (49°C and 60°C), stirring in beeswax slowly.

4. Remove olive oil mixture from heat. Add lye mixture to olive oil mixture, stirring slowly and trying not to splash.

5. Stir occasionally, every 15 minutes or so, until the mixture thickens and congeals. (It will have a texture similar to that of light mayonnaise.)

6. Stir in lemon zest and essential oil. Stir for 1 minute with a spoon (or with a whisk, taking care not to create foam).

7. Pour into a greased or paper-lined soap mold. Gently tap mold to remove any air bubbles.

8. Cover with a blanket or towel and let stand for 2 days. Uncover and let stand for an additional day if the mold is very large.

9. Turn soap out of mold. Wait another day, then cut into bars as desired.

10. Dry bars for 1 month, turning occasionally to ensure they are drying uniformly.

Lemon Soap's Action on the Skin

- This soap has a very positive effect on oily skin.

- It also regulates combination skin, in which the forehead, nose and chin have excess oil while the cheeks exhibit dryness. When applied to the face, this soap does double duty: it fights oil while it softens drier areas.

- If you have varicose veins on your legs, you can gently rub the soap over those areas. It will give them a feeling of well-being and take away the tingling.

- I would especially advise you to wash cuts or abrasions with lemon soap. The soap is also great as a mosquito repellent and a salve for mosquito bites. The itch you'll experience the morning after will be lessened if you use this soap.

COCONUT SOAP

A Tropical Bath

The coconut is the fruit of a palm tree (*Cocos nucifera*) originally from the Americas, although it flourishes in quite a few places around the world.

Many derivatives are extracted from this palm, such as the oil, which is used in cosmetics and cooking, and, of course, the famous coconut milk. Coconut butter, called copra oil, is emulsified to give it a milky appearance. The pulp of the trunk is also edible; it tastes similar to asparagus.

For this soap, you'll need fresh coconut water. A few coconuts will be enough for the recipe. To extract the water without any problem, make a hole with a sharp-tipped knife in one of the small eyes on the coconut. When the hole is large enough, dig deeper with a metal knitting needle. (The hole can also be made with a screwdriver.) After the water has been extracted, strain it to remove any impurities.

Cocoa butter is very easy to find, so it is called for in this recipe, but if you can find coconut butter, it's also a wonderful additive.

Finally, the coconut extract used in this recipe is the type sold for use in cooking.

Coconut Soap

Coconut oil is relaxing for the mind and body, and is ideal for oily skin.

Fun Facts

Sweet coconut water is the reserve that feeds the coconut seed as it germinates.

Coconut oil contains lauric acid (which is also found in human breast milk), which has certain restructuring properties that protect skin and make it soft. It's also an antiseptic and maintains healthy pH levels in the skin.

Note: Exact measurements are crucial in soap making. Turn to page 21 for how-tos.

7.5 oz	coconut water	213 g
3 oz	lye (caustic soda)	85 g
1.5 lbs	extra virgin olive oil	682 g
3 oz	pure cocoa butter	85 g
20	drops coconut extract	20
1 tbsp	desiccated coconut	15 mL
1 tbsp	confectioners' (icing) sugar	15 mL
0.9 oz	coconut oil	25 g

1. Wearing gloves and goggles, pour coconut water into a large saucepan. Add lye slowly, stirring gently until it is dissolved.

2. Using a thermometer, monitor the temperature of the lye mixture until it is between 120°F and 140°F (49°C and 60°C).

3. Meanwhile, in a separate saucepan, heat olive oil to between 120°F and 140°F (49°C and 60°C).

4. Remove olive oil from heat. Add lye mixture to olive oil, stirring slowly and trying not to splash.

5. Stir occasionally, every 15 minutes or so, until the mixture thickens and congeals. (It will have a texture similar to that of light mayonnaise.)

6. Stir in cocoa butter, coconut extract, desiccated coconut, confectioners' sugar and coconut oil. Stir for 1 minute with a spoon (or with a whisk, taking care not to create foam).

7. Pour into a greased or paper-lined soap mold. Gently tap mold to remove any air bubbles.

8. Cover with a blanket or towel and let stand for 2 days. Uncover and let stand for an additional day if the mold is very large.

9. Turn soap out of mold. Wait another day, then cut into bars as desired.

10. Dry bars for 1 month, turning occasionally to ensure they are drying uniformly.

Coconut Soap's Action on the Skin

- ✿ Coconut oil is ideal for oily skin, whether it is acne-prone or not. Not all people who have problems with oiliness have acne or pimples.

- ✿ This soap is definitely not for people who have dry or sensitive skin, because coconut reduces oil and can be excessively drying. Despite its pleasant smell, it shouldn't be used on children.

- ✿ Because this soap includes desiccated coconut among its ingredients, you can use it as an exfoliant, rubbing it gently over oily areas.

- ✿ It's a good idea to moisturize the skin after washing with this soap.

MALLOW SOAP

The Sun in the Evening

The common mallow (*Malva sylvestris*) belongs to the Malvaceae family. It is a plant with very showy, eye-catching flowers.

The parts of the plant used for cosmetics are the flowers and leaves. There is normally no problem finding dried mallow flowers at an herbalist's shop. Finding fresh mallow flowers is more difficult. The only way is to grow them yourself; however, they are easy to grow in pots and have a bountiful yield.

This soap, made with mallow flowers, is a delight that caresses your skin. There are people who don't like the look of the flowers embedded in the soap; the lye can sometimes change their color. I personally find this aversion odd, because when you add an extra ingredient, you never know what color it will be in the end. Plus, when you make a soap recipe several times—even though you add the very same ingredients—it does not come out the same every time. I often prepare bay leaf soap, and I never get the same color twice. Sometimes it takes on brownish tones; other times, greenish ones.

When you make soap with flowers, during the maturation period, you will see a faded halo encircle the flowers. This is created by the essential oils released by the flowers and leaves, which remain in the soap and add their properties to it. It is more noticeable when fresh, rather than dried, flowers are added.

Mallow Soap

Mallow is a powerful anti-inflammatory and softening agent that soothes tissues.

Tips

Although you can use it for the entire body, this soap is ideal for the face.

To make the mallow infusion, in a bowl, pour 7.5 oz (213 g) boiling water over 1 tbsp (15 mL) chopped mallow flower petals. Cover and let stand for 5 minutes. Strain and weigh for recipe.

• • •

Fun Fact

Mallow is a medicinal plant that is taken for bronchitis and made into a gargle for sore throats. It is also applied to the skin as a poultice to treat skin diseases.

Note: Exact measurements are crucial in soap making. Turn to page 21 for how-tos.

7.5 oz	mallow infusion (see tips, at left)	213 g
3 oz	lye (caustic soda)	85 g
1.5 lbs	extra virgin olive oil	682 g
1 tbsp	mallow flowers	15 mL
20	drops mint essential oil	20

1. Wearing gloves and goggles, pour mallow infusion into a large saucepan. Add lye slowly, stirring gently until it is dissolved.

2. Using a thermometer, monitor the temperature of the lye mixture until it is between 120°F and 140°F (49°C and 60°C).

3. Meanwhile, in a separate saucepan, heat olive oil to between 120°F and 140°F (49°C and 60°C).

4. Remove olive oil from heat. Add lye mixture to olive oil, stirring slowly and trying not to splash.

5. Stir occasionally, every 15 minutes or so, until the mixture thickens and congeals. (It will have a texture similar to that of light mayonnaise.)

6. Stir in mallow flowers and essential oil. Stir for 1 minute with a spoon (or with a whisk, taking care not to create any foam).

7. Pour into a greased or paper-lined soap mold. Gently tap mold to remove any air bubbles.

8. Cover with a blanket or towel and let stand for 2 days. Uncover and let stand for an additional day if the mold is very large.

9. Turn soap out of mold. Wait another day, then cut into bars as desired.

10. Dry bars for 1 month, turning occasionally to ensure they are drying uniformly.

Mallow Soap's Action on the Skin

- ❧ This soap has anti-inflammatory properties for skin. It also acts beneficially by cleansing skin of impurities.

- ❧ Due to its gentleness, it is beneficial for all people, including those with sensitive skin.

- ❧ Mallow soap should be kept in a well-drained soap dish. If you leave the soap in contact with moisture, the flowers will take on a somewhat slimy feel.

- ❧ You can use mallow soap for the entire body like other soaps, but it is ideal for the face.

ROSEMARY SOAP

Natural Balance

Rosemary (*Rosmarinus officinalis*) belongs to the Lamiaceae family. It is very popular in Spain, where so much rosemary grew that seafarers could detect the Iberian Peninsula by its aroma before they could see land. Rosemary has been used in folk remedies for centuries. It is abundant throughout the Mediterranean region, where, traditionally, it is used in both cooking and aromatherapy.

Rosemary has always had an aura of mysticism around it, and in ancient times, it was very common to make offerings of the herb in temples. This tradition has survived to this day. The Arabs perfumed and disinfected their bodies after bathing by striking themselves with rosemary branches.

For this soap, you will use rosemary leaves and flowers. I recommend you add fresh ones, as they are not very difficult to find. If it isn't possible, buy the dried version at an herbalist's shop, where it is sold in packages.

There are two kinds of rosemary essential oil: one obtained from fresh flowers, which is of superior quality, and one obtained from the whole plant. Use the one made from flowers for this soap.

Rosemary soap is ideal for treating seborrhea, which causes hair loss in adults. It's also beneficial for babies, who often get little scabs on their scalp. If you wash your hair with this soap, remember that, no matter how natural it is, it stings just like normal shampoo if it comes into contact with your eyes.

Rosemary Soap

This heavenly smelling soap is an excellent skin disinfectant. The essence of rosemary is also very agreeable and works especially well with lemon.

Tips

Rosemary is such a powerful herb that it should not be used during the first trimester of pregnancy.

To make the rosemary infusion, in a bowl, pour 7.5 oz (213 g) boiling water over 1 tbsp (15 mL) crushed rosemary. Cover and let stand for 5 minutes. Strain and weigh for recipe.

Note: Exact measurements are crucial in soap making. Turn to page 21 for how-tos.

7.5 oz	rosemary infusion (see tips, at left)	213 g
3 oz	lye (caustic soda)	85 g
1.5 lbs	extra virgin olive oil	682 g
1 tbsp	rosemary leaves or flowers	15 mL
0.15 oz	rosemary essential oil	4 g

1. Wearing gloves and goggles, pour rosemary infusion into a large saucepan. Add lye slowly, stirring gently until it is dissolved.

2. Using a thermometer, monitor the temperature of the lye mixture until it is between 120°F and 140°F (49°C and 60°C).

3. Meanwhile, in a separate saucepan, heat olive oil to between 120°F and 140°F (49°C and 60°C).

4. Remove olive oil from heat. Add lye mixture to olive oil, stirring slowly and trying not to splash.

5. Stir occasionally, every 15 minutes or so, until the mixture thickens and congeals. (It will have a texture similar to that of light mayonnaise.)

6. Stir in rosemary leaves and essential oil. Stir for 1 minute with a spoon (or with a whisk, taking care not to create any foam).

7. Pour into a greased or paper-lined soap mold. Gently tap mold to remove any air bubbles.

8. Cover with a blanket or towel and let stand for 2 days. Uncover and let stand for an additional day if the mold is very large.

9. Turn soap out of mold. Wait another day, then cut into bars as desired.

10. Dry bars for 1 month, turning occasionally to ensure they are drying uniformly.

Rosemary Soap's Action on the Skin

- This soap is a skin disinfectant. It fights acne, dermatitis, eczema and any problem caused by excess oil production.

- Keep in mind that rosemary essential oil is contraindicated in people with epilepsy; those who suffer from this condition should avoid it. Pregnant women should also avoid using rosemary essential oil. In both cases, refrain from using this soap.

- Otherwise, this is a wonderful soap with a multitude of virtues.

MARIGOLD SOAP

The Flower that Heals Wounds

The calendula (*Calendula officinalis*) is a member of the Asteraceae family and is also known as the marigold and the flower of the dead. It has countless properties, whether the plant is used internally or externally. Here, I will focus on its properties that benefit skin.

When mixed with a carrier oil, such as sweet almond oil, marigold essential oil is beneficial for hemorrhoids and stretch marks, especially those produced by pregnancy. Recent stretch marks are easier to mitigate than those resulting from weight loss, which may have existed for a longer time.

The marigold flower is showy and has an intense, yellow-orange color. Its essential oil is extracted from the flowers, which are easy to grow. Look for the seeds at nurseries and large shopping centers. Plant some in a medium-size planter and place it outside. One planter will yield enough flowers to cover all your needs. Marigold petals are antibacterial, anti-inflammatory and astringent; they are used on ulcers, burns, inflammation, cracked skin, insect bites and more.

I call the marigold "the mature woman's flower." It is beneficial for mature skin no matter how it is used. If you make an infusion of petals and store it in the refrigerator, you can apply the tonic in the morning. The result is spectacular and leaves skin smooth, with a feeling of freshness. It also fights wrinkles when used in soaps and creams.

Marigold Soap

Tip

To make the marigold infusion, in a bowl, pour 7.5 oz (213 g) boiling water over 1 tbsp (15 mL) marigold petals. Cover and let stand for 5 minutes. Strain and weigh for recipe.

• • •

Fun Facts

Calendulas, or marigolds, bloom every month. Hence, their name comes from *calendae,* the first day of every month in ancient Rome.

Marigold flowers, which are antiseptic and healing, are thrown on graves on All Saints' Day.

Note: Exact measurements are crucial in soap making. Turn to page 21 for how-tos.

7.5 oz	marigold infusion (see tip, at left)	213 g
3 oz	lye (caustic soda)	85 g
1.5 lbs	extra virgin olive oil	682 g
0.35 oz	beeswax	10 g
1 tbsp	marigold petals	15 mL
0.07 oz	marigold essential oil	2 g

1. Wearing gloves and goggles, pour marigold infusion into a large saucepan. Add lye slowly, stirring gently until it is dissolved.

2. Using a thermometer, monitor the temperature of the lye mixture until it is between 120°F and 140°F (49°C and 60°C).

3. Meanwhile, in a separate saucepan, heat olive oil to between 120°F and 140°F (49°C and 60°C), stirring in beeswax slowly.

4. Remove olive oil mixture from heat. Add lye mixture to olive oil mixture, stirring slowly and trying not to splash.

5. Stir occasionally, every 15 minutes or so, until the mixture thickens and congeals. (It will have a texture similar to that of light mayonnaise.)

6. Stir in marigold petals and essential oil. Stir for 1 minute with a spoon (or with a whisk, taking care not to create any foam).

7. Pour into a greased or paper-lined soap mold. Gently tap mold to remove any air bubbles.

8. Cover with a blanket or towel and let stand for 2 days. Uncover and let stand for an additional day if the mold is very large.

9. Turn soap out of mold. Wait another day, then cut into bars as desired.

10. Dry bars for 1 month, turning occasionally to ensure they are drying uniformly.

Marigold Soap's Action on the Skin

- This soap should be used by people with rashes, wounds, burns and cuts. Men or women who perform manual work and often suffer cuts or other wounds should wash with this soap frequently.

- People who want to keep wrinkles at bay and those who have rough skin should use this soap; they will benefit from the softness it provides.

- As in other soap recipes that call for flowers, you can use either fresh or dried petals for this soap.

SAGE SOAP

The Doctor in the Garden

Spanish sage (*Salvia lavandulifolia*) belongs to the Lamiaceae family, like common sage (*Salvia officinalis*) and clary sage (*Salvia sclarea*). Although these different sages belong to the same family, each has its own particular characteristics, not only in appearance but also in therapeutic properties.

For this soap, use Spanish sage leaves and flowers (dried or fresh), and Spanish sage essential oil. When buying essential oil, be careful not to confuse sages, because, for instance, *Salvia officinalis* has some major contraindications.

Spanish sage is so named because it is native to the Iberian Peninsula, where it has traditionally been used to treat all kinds of ailments, including colds, headaches, flu, coughs, rheumatism, mouth infections and more.

I would especially like to emphasize this soap's beneficial action against excessive perspiration. It does not prevent the body's normal and regular perspiration, which is beneficial, but rather acts when sweating gets excessive.

Sage soap also has the virtue of minimizing body odor. If odor is very persistent, you can apply compresses soaked in sage infusion or in water combined with a few drops of sage essential oil directly to the underarms.

Sage Soap

Tips

Dissolve sage soap in hot water and gradually add two beaten eggs to create a beneficial shampoo.

To make the sage infusion, in a bowl, pour 7.5 oz (213 g) boiling water over 1 tbsp (15 mL) sage leaves and flowers. Cover and let stand for 5 minutes. Strain and weigh for recipe.

• • •

Fun Facts

Salvia lavandulifolia grows on limestone surfaces, especially in southern Spain.

The name *Salvia* comes from the Latin word *salvere*, which means "to heal or cure."

Note: Exact measurements are crucial in soap making. Turn to page 21 for how-tos.

7.5 oz	sage infusion (see tips, at left)	213 g
3 oz	lye (caustic soda)	85 g
1.5 lbs	extra virgin olive oil	682 g
0.18 oz	beeswax	5 g
0.18 oz	pure cocoa butter	5 g
0.18 oz	Spanish sage essential oil	5 g

1. Wearing gloves and goggles, pour sage infusion into a large saucepan. Add lye slowly, stirring gently until it is dissolved.

2. Using a thermometer, monitor the temperature of the lye mixture until it is between 120°F and 140°F (49°C and 60°C).

3. Meanwhile, in a separate saucepan, heat olive oil to between 120°F and 140°F (49°C and 60°C), stirring in beeswax slowly.

4. Remove olive oil mixture from heat. Add lye mixture to olive oil mixture, stirring slowly and trying not to splash.

5. Stir occasionally, every 15 minutes or so, until the mixture thickens and congeals. (It will have a texture similar to that of light mayonnaise.)

6. Stir in cocoa butter and essential oil. Stir for 1 minute with a spoon (or with a whisk, taking care not to create any foam).

7. Pour into a greased or paper-lined soap mold. Gently tap mold to remove any air bubbles.

8. Cover with a blanket or towel and let stand for 2 days. Uncover and let stand for an additional day if the mold is very large.

9. Turn soap out of mold. Wait another day, then cut into bars as desired.

10. Dry bars for 1 month, turning occasionally to ensure they are drying uniformly.

Sage Soap's Action on the Skin

- ✣ Sage soap performs a wide range of activities, including fighting acne, treating sensitive skin, mitigating dermatitis and, as already mentioned, helping reduce excessive perspiration.

- ✣ This soap is also good for dandruff. If you want to use it as a shampoo substitute (see tips, opposite), you'll be fine if you alternate with your usual shampoo.

- ✣ Sage soap also works well for people with fair complexions and those who have sensitive skin.

CHAMOMILE SOAP

The Mildest Soothing Soap

Roman chamomile (*Chamaemelum nobile*) belongs to the Asteraceae family. It is also known as English chamomile. There are many varieties of chamomile worldwide; the most commonly used is Roman chamomile, because it has the largest number of healing properties.

Chamomile was being used more than 2,500 years ago by a variety of cultures in the Mediterranean region. Its essential oil is extracted from its delicate white flowers.

Chamomile is used widely in the food industry, in some medicines and especially in cosmetics. The king of all products is chamomile-based shampoo, as well as hair lightening lotion.

In some areas of Spain, there is a tradition of drinking chamomile tea before bedtime, especially among older people, because chamomile exerts an analgesic and soporific effect. Young children are also given teaspoons of chamomile tea when they have indigestion.

For this soap, we will use fresh or dried Roman chamomile. You will also need Roman chamomile essential oil and ylang-ylang essential oil, which blends well with chamomile. In addition to its many wellness-enhancing properties, ylang-ylang has a delicate and subtle aroma.

Chamomile Soap

Tips

The use of chamomile is not recommended in the first trimester of pregnancy.

To make the Roman chamomile infusion, in a bowl, pour 7.5 oz (213 g) boiling water over 2 tbsp (30 mL) Roman chamomile. Cover and let stand for 5 minutes. Strain and weigh for recipe.

• • •

Fun Fact

In San Juan Mirador in Guatemala, women prepare chamomile soap in May by mixing sheets of soap with chamomile tea. They then sell the soap at the market.

Note: Exact measurements are crucial in soap making. Turn to page 21 for how-tos.

7.5 oz	Roman chamomile infusion (see tips, at left)	213 g
3 oz	lye (caustic soda)	85 g
1.5 lbs	extra virgin olive oil	682 g
0.35 oz	pure cocoa butter	10 g
0.07 oz	Roman chamomile essential oil	2 g
0.07 oz	ylang-ylang essential oil	2 g

1. Wearing gloves and goggles, pour chamomile infusion into a large saucepan. Add lye slowly, stirring gently until it is dissolved.

2. Using a thermometer, monitor the temperature of the lye mixture until it is between 120°F and 140°F (49°C and 60°C).

3. Meanwhile, in a separate saucepan, heat olive oil to between 120°F and 140°F (49°C and 60°C).

4. Remove olive oil from heat. Add lye mixture to olive oil, stirring slowly and trying not to splash.

5. Stir occasionally, every 15 minutes or so, until the mixture thickens and congeals. (It will have a texture similar to that of light mayonnaise.)

6. Stir in cocoa butter, and chamomile and ylang-ylang essential oils. Stir for 1 minute with a spoon (or with a whisk, taking care not to create foam).

7. Pour into a greased or paper-lined soap mold. Gently tap mold to remove any air bubbles.

8. Cover with a blanket or towel and let stand for 2 days. Uncover and let stand for an additional day if the mold is very large.

9. Turn soap out of mold. Wait another day, then cut into bars as desired.

10. Dry bars for 1 month, turning occasionally to ensure they are drying uniformly.

Chamomile Soap's Action on the Skin

- If there is a quintessential olive oil soap for sensitive skin, it's chamomile soap. It is ideal for children, the elderly and people who are prone to skin sensitivity, skin allergies and rashes.

- This soap is best if you use it on your face, where it softens and rebalances. In any case, I advise you to always moisturize the skin well after showering or washing your face with soap.

- From experience, I know that a soap or gel always alters the skin pH, no matter how mild it is. To rebalance it, apply oil or a gentle cream.

CHOCOLATE SOAP

The Romantic Option

Cocoa (*Theobroma cacao*) belongs to the Sterculiaceae family. It is a tree native to the Americas but now grows elsewhere. The fruit is a large pod of the same name: cocoa.

Various products are extracted from cocoa pods, including cocoa powder, which is made by toasting and grinding the beans that grow inside the pod. Often this powder has the oils removed and is made by grinding the cocoa solids.

An oil called theobroma is also produced. It is widely used in the baking industry and also in cosmetics, for manufacturing everything from creams to lipsticks. Cocoa butter is produced from this oil.

The addition of cocoa powder to cosmetics is relatively new and somewhat exotic, but it is very effective. Today, there are all kinds of cocoa-based treatments. There are therapeutic body massages for water retention and cellulitis, facials for deep nourishment and hair treatments.

Use 100% pure cocoa powder for this soap. Don't use sweetened cocoa powder used to flavor milk, because this mixture includes a ridiculous amount of other unwanted substances. The cocoa butter that you add to the soap must be pure, too; it is not difficult to find at specialty shops or even pharmacies.

Chocolate Soap

Open a sultry gateway to the world of the senses. This soap nourishes and moisturizes deeply.

Fun Fact

Chocolate baths have become popular. They are soothing and comforting, and have an erotic component that makes them ideal. You'll quickly discover why chocolate soap is sold at adult stores.

Note: Exact measurements are crucial in soap making. Turn to page 21 for how-tos.

7.5 oz	mineral water	213 g
3 oz	lye (caustic soda)	85 g
1.5 lbs	extra virgin olive oil	682 g
1.8 oz	pure cocoa butter	50 g
1 tbsp	pure cocoa powder	15 mL
0.18 oz	orange essential oil	5 g

1. Wearing gloves and goggles, pour mineral water into a large saucepan. Add lye slowly, stirring gently until it is dissolved.

2. Using a thermometer, monitor the temperature of the lye mixture until it is between 120°F and 140°F (49°C and 60°C).

3. Meanwhile, in a separate saucepan, heat olive oil to between 120°F and 140°F (49°C and 60°C).

4. Remove olive oil from heat. Add lye mixture to olive oil, stirring slowly and trying not to splash.

5. Stir occasionally, every 15 minutes or so, until the mixture thickens and congeals. (It will have a texture similar to that of light mayonnaise.)

6. Stir in cocoa butter, cocoa powder and essential oil. Stir for 1 minute with a spoon (or with a whisk, taking care not to create foam).

7. Pour into a greased or paper-lined soap mold. Gently tap mold to remove any air bubbles.

8. Cover with a blanket or towel and let stand for 2 days. Uncover and let stand for an additional day if the mold is very large.

9. Turn soap out of mold. Wait another day, then cut into bars as desired.

10. Dry bars for 1 month, turning occasionally to ensure they are drying uniformly.

Chocolate Soap's Action on the Skin

- If you massage this soap over the skin every day in areas affected by water retention or cellulitis, you will notice a positive effect after just a few weeks.

- Chocolate soap nourishes skin and moisturizes it deeply. It is very purifying for people who do hard physical labor, which can make the skin suffer.

- Due to its vitamin C content—thanks to the orange essential oil that infuses it—this soap also encourages sebaceous regulation.

- You may also use this soap as a body mask. Moisten the skin, apply the soap over the entire body and let it stand for 5 minutes before rinsing it off with water. It will simultaneously give the effects of a smoothing peel and a mask.

ROSE SOAP

The Most Delicate Scent

The cabbage rose (*Rosa centifolia*) belongs to the Rosaceae family and has many names, including Roman rose and hundred-leaved rose.

Another variety that can be used to make soap is the damask rose, or rose of Castile (*Rosa damascena*). It even has some properties that are superior to those of the cabbage rose.

The rose is native to Asia but is now cultivated throughout the world. There are about 11,000 varieties of roses, and although all have some characteristics in common, some varieties possess certain inherent qualities that make them uniquely suited to specific treatments. The rose has been used to cure all kinds of ailments, from headaches to circulatory problems.

In cosmetics, roses are one of the most used plants. They are the basis of the eternally famous rose water, rose floral water, perfumes, soaps and cosmetics.

For this soap, you will need rose water and rose petals, either fresh or dried. The only thing you need to keep in mind when working with those petals is that they shouldn't have been sprayed with pesticides or herbicides, because those unwanted products will spoil your soap. Ideally, you should grow your own rose bush to ensure that it is not sprayed.

You will also need rose fragrance or rose herbal distillate. Rose essential oil is best, but there is a problem: It is very scarce and prohibitively expensive. That's why I recommend herbal distillate or fragrance, despite the fact that it is sometimes artificial and can contain a mixture of essential oils and alcohol.

Rose Soap

Delicate rose soap is exceptional for wrinkled and aging skin.

Fun Facts

Rose water is made from *Rosa centifolia* petals. To create 2 cups (500 mL) of this water, you need to distill the petals from more than 1,000 flowers. Rose water may be used in cooking or as a condiment.

The Grasse rose (a type of centifolia rose grown in France) produces, through extraction of distillates, an almost perfect rose essence.

Note: Exact measurements are crucial in soap making. Turn to page 21 for how-tos.

7.5 oz	rose water	213 g
3 oz	lye (caustic soda)	85 g
1.5 lbs	extra virgin olive oil	682 g
0.35 oz	beeswax	10 g
1 tbsp	rose petals	15 mL
0.35 oz	rose fragrance or rose herbal distillate	10 g

1. Wearing gloves and goggles, pour rose water into a large saucepan. Add lye slowly, stirring gently until it is dissolved.

2. Using a thermometer, monitor the temperature of the lye mixture until it is between 120°F and 140°F (49°C and 60°C).

3. Meanwhile, in a separate saucepan, heat olive oil to between 120°F and 140°F (49°C and 60°C), stirring in beeswax slowly.

4. Remove olive oil mixture from heat. Add lye mixture to olive oil mixture, stirring slowly and trying not to splash.

5. Stir occasionally, every 15 minutes or so, until the mixture thickens and congeals. (It will have a texture similar to that of light mayonnaise.)

6. Stir in rose petals and fragrance. Stir for 1 minute with a spoon (or with a whisk, taking care not to create foam).

7. Pour into a greased or paper-lined soap mold. Gently tap mold to remove any air bubbles.

8. Cover with a blanket or towel and let stand for 2 days. Uncover and let stand for an additional day if the mold is very large.

9. Turn soap out of mold. Wait another day, then cut into bars as desired.

10. Dry bars for 1 month, turning occasionally to ensure they are drying uniformly.

Rose Soap's Action on the Skin

- ❧ Rose soap is highly recommended for people who have dry or sensitive skin, or wrinkles.

- ❧ This soap is also recommended for skin that is sensitive to changes in temperature, like those that occur in summer with air conditioning, and in winter with heating and ambient indoor dryness.

- ❧ If you have skin that is not sensitive, temperature contrasts won't affect you much. But if you do, you should take precautions to protect it by using nourishing soaps and creams.

LAVENDER SOAP

The Aroma of the Mediterranean

Lavender (*Lavandula officinalis*) belongs to the Lamiaceae family. Light purple flowers are most common, but there is a variety that produces white flowers.

Lavender is native to the Mediterranean. It is quite popular and is grown throughout the world for its aroma, which seemingly everyone likes. It is not uncommon to keep a bag of dried lavender flowers in the closet to make your clothes smell good.

The therapeutic effects of lavender are quite diverse: it is an antiseptic and anti-rheumatic, acts as a deodorant, and is also used to treat sprains and throat infections.

Lavender and its essential oil are widely used in drug making (to prepare ointments and lotions) and in cosmetics (to prepare creams, mouthwashes, perfumes and colognes).

Lavender essential oil is important because it soothes many ailments. It has been shown to be useful in healing burns, insect bites, wounds, cystitis and a long list of other maladies.

For this soap, use the entire stem with its flowers (fresh or dried) to make the infusion and as an extra ingredient. You will also need lavender essential oil, which, besides giving the soap its distinctive aroma, adds health-enhancing properties.

If you like, when the soap is placed in the mold, decorate it with green lavender leaves.

Lavender Soap

Tip

To make the lavender infusion, in a bowl, pour 7.5 oz (213 g) boiling water over 2 tbsp (30 mL) fresh or dried lavender. Cover and let stand for 5 minutes. Strain and weigh for recipe.

• • •

Fun Facts

Lavender contains up to 3% essential oil, which is very much coveted in perfumery.

Rubbing the skin with lavender-infused alcohol reactivates circulation and relieves fatigue. Macerated in water, lavender is a digestive.

Note: Exact measurements are crucial in soap making. Turn to page 21 for how-tos.

7.5 oz	lavender infusion (see tip, at left)	213 g
3 oz	lye (caustic soda)	85 g
1.5 lbs	extra virgin olive oil	682 g
1 tbsp	fresh or dried lavender	15 mL
0.35 oz	lavender essential oil	10 g

1. Wearing gloves and goggles, pour lavender infusion into a large saucepan. Add lye slowly, stirring gently until it is dissolved.

2. Using a thermometer, monitor the temperature of the lye mixture until it is between 120°F and 140°F (49°C and 60°C).

3. Meanwhile, in a separate saucepan, heat olive oil to between 120°F and 140°F (49°C and 60°C).

4. Remove olive oil from heat. Add lye mixture to olive oil, stirring slowly and trying not to splash.

5. Stir occasionally, every 15 minutes or so, until the mixture thickens and congeals. (It will have a texture similar to that of light mayonnaise.)

6. Stir in lavender and essential oil. Stir for 1 minute with a spoon (or with a whisk, taking care not to create foam).

7. Pour into a greased or paper-lined soap mold. Gently tap mold to remove any air bubbles.

8. Cover with a blanket or towel and let stand for 2 days. Uncover and let stand for an additional day if the mold is very large.

9. Turn soap out of mold. Wait another day, then cut into bars as desired.

10. Dry bars for 1 month, turning occasionally to ensure they are drying uniformly.

Lavender Soap's Action on the Skin

- Lavender soap is great for children, but it is also good for elderly people, whose skin gradually loses its elasticity and natural defenses. Lavender soap is antiseptic and protects skin from infections, eczema and more.

- Lavender soap also fights psoriasis, by attenuating the scaly appearance that this disease gives the skin.

- To treat a boil, apply lavender soap to it and let it dry for half an hour. Then remove the soap with a water-soaked sponge. This helps the boil mature and brings the infection up to the surface of the skin.

MARSHMALLOW SOAP

The Sweet Smell of Childhood

The common marshmallow (*Althaea officinalis*) belongs to the Malvaceae family. It grows around the globe, in damp areas such as swamps, bogs and ponds.

The most-used parts of the plant are its leaves and roots. They all have a similar function and can be used internally, in the form of infusions and decoctions, or externally, in the form of poultices and compresses.

Mallow is a very mucilage-rich plant, which makes it an excellent emollient. In other words, it serves to soften and relax inflamed body parts. For this soap, unlike others, you will use the dried leaves and roots. If you collect the roots yourself, they must be dried immediately once plucked, free of any sand and rootlets. Use the roots to make the infusion, and the marshmallow leaves as an extra ingredient.

Note that we will prepare the root infusion according to the recipe of Dioscorides, the famous Roman physician of the 1st century AD, without letting the water come to a boil. It should be hot, but your hand should be able to withstand the heat.

We will also use beeswax to help harden the soap and to add the numerous nutrients that it contains. Ylang-ylang essential oil, which is also added to this soap, will provide its signature fragrance and its virtues as the perfect skin restructurer.

Marshmallow Soap

Marshmallow mucilage is the best remedy for skin inflammations. It also softens and heals skin lesions very effectively.

Tip

To make the marshmallow infusion, in a bowl, pour 7.5 oz (213 g) boiling water over 2 tbsp (30 mL) dried marshmallow roots. Cover and let stand for 5 minutes. Strain and weigh for recipe.

• • •

Fun Fact

Marshmallow flowers are the color of a cloud of sugar. When mucilage extracted from the root was mixed with beaten egg white, gum arabic, flavoring, cornstarch and powdered sugar, it produced the original marshmallow candy.

Note: Exact measurements are crucial in soap making. Turn to page 21 for how-tos.

7.5 oz	marshmallow infusion (see tip, at left)	213 g
3 oz	lye (caustic soda)	85 g
1.5 lbs	extra virgin olive oil	682 g
0.35 oz	beeswax	10 g
1 tbsp	chopped marshmallow leaves	15 mL
0.18 oz	ylang-ylang essential oil	5 g

1. Wearing gloves and goggles, pour marshmallow infusion into a large saucepan. Add lye slowly, stirring gently until dissolved.

2. Using a thermometer, monitor the temperature of the lye mixture until it is between 120°F and 140°F (49°C and 60°C).

3. Meanwhile, in a separate saucepan, heat olive oil to between 120°F and 140°F (49°C and 60°C), stirring in beeswax slowly.

4. Remove olive oil mixture from heat. Add lye mixture to olive oil mixture, stirring slowly and trying not to splash.

5. Stir occasionally, every 15 minutes or so, until the mixture thickens and congeals. (It will have a texture similar to that of light mayonnaise.)

6. Stir in marshmallow leaves and essential oil. Stir for 1 minute with a spoon (or with a whisk, taking care not to create foam).

7. Pour into a greased or paper-lined soap mold. Gently tap mold to remove any air bubbles.

8. Cover with a blanket or towel and let stand for 2 days. Uncover and let stand for an additional day if the mold is very large.

9. Turn soap out of mold. Wait another day, then cut into bars as desired.

10. Dry bars for 1 month, turning occasionally to ensure they are drying uniformly.

Marshmallow Soap's Action on the Skin

- ❦ This soap has a soothing, softening effect on all types of young and not-so-young skin.

- ❦ It also does wonders for people with skin ulcers. Apply the soap to the affected area and leave it to dry for five minutes. Then rinse it off with water.

- ❦ Like all olive oil soaps, marshmallow soap should be kept in a dish with grooves or a grate so that it stays well ventilated. If you leave it in a dish in which water pools, the soap will get soft and you will use it up much more quickly.

CINNAMON SOAP

Warm and Intoxicating

The cinnamon tree (*Cinnamomum zeylanicum*) belongs to the Lauraceae family. The cinnamon sticks that we're all familiar with are extracted from the inner part of the bark on the tree's youngest branches.

Although cinnamon grows in several countries, cinnamon par excellence comes from Madagascar and is known for its fineness and fragrance. The tree is so aromatic that just touching the leaves will saturate your hands with the plant's intoxicating scent.

What catches your attention most about cinnamon is its unmistakable aroma. However, it also has interesting therapeutic properties; for instance, as an antiseptic for the mouth, teeth and gums. There are cinnamon mouthwashes on the market created just for this purpose.

The cinnamon tree produces two types of essential oil: one is extracted from the tree's bark, which is irritating to the skin; the other is extracted from the leaves and twigs, which must be used in moderation. Cinnamon leaf essential oil is used in cosmetics and perfumery, and has many applications in the food industry.

For this soap, you will use ground cinnamon for its scent, color and health-enhancing properties. You'll also add a small amount of cinnamon leaf essential oil, plus cocoa butter to soften and moisturize the skin.

Cinnamon Soap

In addition to offering its warm, spicy scent, cinnamon is an antiseptic, a stimulant and an aphrodisiac.

Fun Facts

Cinnamon is used with bamboo in Chi Yang massage to firm the skin and eliminate cellulite.

It is believed that cinnamon, which originated in Ceylon (now Sri Lanka), arrived in Egypt via China more than 4,000 years ago. It later became one of the most prized and expensive spices of ancient times.

In ancient Egypt, cinnamon and myrrh were part of a perfume called Mendesian.

Note: Exact measurements are crucial in soap making. Turn to page 21 for how-tos.

7.5 oz	mineral water	213 g
3 oz	lye (caustic soda)	85 g
1.5 lbs	extra virgin olive oil	682 g
0.35 oz	pure cocoa butter	10 g
1 tbsp	ground cinnamon	15 mL
0.07 oz	cinnamon leaf essential oil	2 g

1. Wearing gloves and goggles, pour mineral water into a large saucepan. Add lye slowly, stirring gently until it is dissolved.

2. Using a thermometer, monitor the temperature of the lye mixture until it is between 120°F and 140°F (49°C and 60°C).

3. Meanwhile, in a separate saucepan, heat olive oil to between 120°F and 140°F (49°C and 60°C).

4. Remove olive oil from heat. Add lye mixture to olive oil, stirring slowly and trying not to splash.

5. Stir occasionally, every 15 minutes or so, until the mixture thickens and congeals. (It will have a texture similar to that of light mayonnaise.)

6. Stir in cocoa butter, ground cinnamon and essential oil. Stir for 1 minute with a spoon (or with a whisk, taking care not to create foam).

7. Pour into a greased or paper-lined soap mold. Gently tap mold to remove any air bubbles.

8. Cover with a blanket or towel and let stand for 2 days. Uncover and let stand for an additional day if the mold is very large.

9. Turn soap out of mold. Wait another day, then cut into bars as desired.

10. Dry bars for 1 month, turning occasionally to ensure they are drying uniformly.

Cinnamon Soap's Action on the Skin

- ❧ The main feature of cinnamon soap is its antiseptic power. It is very important for a soap to have this ability, because the skin is exposed to all sorts of attacks every day.

- ❧ I think this soap is ideal as a beauty or hand soap.

- ❧ Children often come in from outdoors with their hands so dirty you can hardly believe it. Well, that situation calls for this type of soap. It is also ideal for adults who have been performing especially dirty manual labor or for chefs or food handlers, who need to touch food with clean hands.

CLOVE SOAP

The Queen of Spices

Cloves (*Syzygium aromaticum* or *Eugenia caryophyllata*), belong to the Myrtaceae family. Though the plant is native to the Moluccas, it is currently grown wherever the climate permits.

The buds of the clove tree, which are harvested before the flowers open, are used in the cuisines of many countries. Cloves are a highly prized spice for cooking due to their intense aroma. They are used in roasts, with game meat and in some fish recipes, especially for baked fish. In perfumery, cloves are used widely in men's colognes because they have a subtle masculine scent. In cosmetics, they are part of numerous formulas for scented creams or soaps.

Different essential oils can be extracted from the clove tree, depending on whether they come from the leaves, trunk or buds. The essential oils extracted from the leaves and trunk should not be used on the skin because they have a high percentage of the compound eugenol, which is irritating.

The essential oil made from the buds is the most prized, but it must be used in moderation. You will add a small amount of it to the soap formula you're going to concoct.

As an extra ingredient, you will add whole buds (whole cloves) or ground cloves. Note that if you use ground cloves, they will not serve as an exfoliant.

Clove Soap

Fun Facts

Clove oil, widely used in aromatherapy, is distilled from the dried unopened flower buds of the clove tree. Thanks to its spicy scent, it is highly regarded in perfumery and is a valuable fragrance in cosmetics.

Cloves prevent contagion and have a long history of fighting off plagues.

Note: Exact measurements are crucial in soap making. Turn to page 21 for how-tos.

7.5 oz	mineral water	213 g
3 oz	lye (caustic soda)	85 g
1.5 lbs	extra virgin olive oil	682 g
0.35 oz	beeswax	10 g
1 tbsp	whole or ground cloves	15 mL
0.07 oz	clove bud essential oil	2 g

1. Wearing gloves and goggles, pour mineral water into a large saucepan. Add lye slowly, stirring gently until it is dissolved.

2. Using a thermometer, monitor the temperature of the lye mixture until it is between 120°F and 140°F (49°C and 60°C).

3. Meanwhile, in a separate saucepan, heat olive oil to between 120°F and 140°F (49°C and 60°C), stirring in beeswax slowly.

4. Remove olive oil mixture from heat. Add lye mixture to olive oil mixture, stirring slowly and trying not to splash.

5. Stir occasionally, every 15 minutes or so, until the mixture thickens and congeals. (It will have a texture similar to that of light mayonnaise.)

6. Stir in cloves and essential oil. Stir for 1 minute with a spoon (or with a whisk, taking care not to create foam).

7. Pour into a greased or paper-lined soap mold. Gently tap mold to remove any air bubbles.

8. Cover with a blanket or towel and let stand for 2 days. Uncover and let stand for an additional day if the mold is very large.

9. Turn soap out of mold. Wait another day, then cut into bars as desired.

10. Dry bars for 1 month, turning occasionally to ensure they are drying uniformly.

Clove Soap's Action on the Skin

- This soap has a very masculine scent, and it improves the appearance of bruises. It is also effective at fighting athlete's foot and is a good antiseptic for wounded skin.

- If you make the soap with whole cloves and rub it in circles directly on the skin, you will benefit from its virtues as an exfoliant. It will also provide relief for poor circulation and tired legs.

- Women also enjoy using this soap, despite its masculine scent.

HONEY SOAP

The Gift of the Bees

Throughout history, honey has been part of everyday life in many cultures, both as food and as medicine. Honey is quite beneficial to the body. It reinforces the immune system, attenuates lung disorders and canker sores, and also tones the heart and increases the number of red blood cells. Used topically, honey helps form scar tissue and soothes red, irritated skin.

There are many types of honey. While they all have features in common, each honey has a specific quality that depends on the plant from which the bees extracted the nectar. Heather honey, for example, is recommended for urinary tract problems. Lavender honey is used for bronchial ailments. Eucalyptus honey is widely acknowledged to be an effective treatment for coughs. And there are many more.

Look for high-quality honey for this soap. The honey we get from large name-brand companies or at major retail outlets is not very good quality and tends to be mixed with other additives in order to cut costs. It is preferable to buy honey directly from a beekeeper or from a small family business. There are also health food stores or farmer's markets where you can buy honey that is difficult to find at conventional outlets. One advantage of honey is that it keeps well, so you can buy it and store it, knowing that it will last for longer than a year.

I want to stress the importance of using superior honey bought from an artisan if possible. While the quality of a single ingredient is not so important in other recipes, in this case, it is essential in order to obtain good-quality soap that has the above-mentioned health-enhancing properties.

Honey Soap

This gentle soap, full of small and creamy bubbles, will never disappoint you.

Tips

Make honey soap in hexagonal molds to imitate the look of honeycombs. For an even lovelier soap, add ground cinnamon and almonds, as desired.

Look for a substance called honeydew, which is produced by bees from the sweet secretions left by other sap-sucking insects. Pine honeydew is very much coveted for its nutritional and therapeutic characteristics.

To make the honey infusion, in a bowl, stir 7.5 oz (213 g) hot water with 1 tbsp (15 mL) liquid honey until dissolved. Weigh for recipe.

Note: Exact measurements are crucial in soap making. Turn to page 21 for how-tos.

7.5 oz	honey infusion (see tips, at left)	213 g
3 oz	lye (caustic soda)	85 g
1.5 lbs	extra virgin olive oil	682 g
0.35 oz	beeswax	10 g
2.1 oz	liquid honey	60 g
0.07 oz	rosemary essential oil	2 g

1. Wearing gloves and goggles, pour honey infusion into a large saucepan. Add lye slowly, stirring gently until it is dissolved.

2. Using a thermometer, monitor the temperature of the lye mixture until it is between 120°F and 140°F (49°C and 60°C).

3. Meanwhile, in a separate saucepan, heat olive oil to between 120°F and 140°F (49°C and 60°C), stirring in beeswax slowly.

4. Remove olive oil mixture from heat. Add lye mixture to olive oil mixture, stirring slowly and trying not to splash.

5. Stir occasionally, every 15 minutes or so, until the mixture thickens and congeals. (It will have a texture similar to that of light mayonnaise.)

6. Stir in honey and essential oil. Stir for 1 minute with a spoon (or with a whisk, taking care not to create foam).

7. Pour into a greased or paper-lined soap mold. Gently tap mold to remove any air bubbles.

8. Cover with a blanket or towel and let stand for 2 days. Uncover and let stand for an additional day if the mold is very large.

9. Turn soap out of mold. Wait another day, then cut into bars as desired.

10. Dry bars for 1 month, turning occasionally to ensure they are drying uniformly.

Honey Soap's Action on the Skin

❧ This soap is useful for all skin types. It is especially beneficial for children and the elderly. Their sensitive skin finds it to be a great ally in soothing any ailments.

❧ Some people's skin does not withstand sudden temperature changes, and they suffer from a striking redness that occurs on the cheeks; some even feel like their faces are burning. Washing with honey soap can help alleviate this disorder.

❧ Honey soap's healing action is increased by the addition of beeswax as an extra ingredient.

COCOA BUTTER SOAP

The Food of the Gods

Cocoa butter is derived from theobroma oil, the natural oil of the cocoa bean (*Theobroma cacao*).

Cocoa butter's melting temperature is very similar to our body temperature. For this reason, it is used to create innumerable creams, ointments, soaps, lipsticks and other cosmetics. Until the middle of the 20th century, it was also an important ingredient used to make suppositories. Cocoa butter is also used in the food industry to make chocolate, cookies and pastries.

Many of the recipes in this book use small quantities of cocoa butter because of its softening power. In the case of this particular soap, however, cocoa butter is the main ingredient. It will yield an extra-gentle soap that's very creamy, with a pleasant scent.

Look for pure cocoa butter at specialty shops and pharmacies. It is sold in bulk, in large chunks. It is one of the most shelf-stable fats around and can be stored for up to three years.

I advise you to grate a large chunk of bulk cocoa butter like this before adding it to the soap mixture. If you grate it, it will be easier to integrate it into the mixture and distribute it evenly.

Vanilla essential oil lends the finished soap an unmistakable, enticing scent.

Cocoa Butter Soap

Cocoa butter is absorbed quickly by the skin and gives it a highly appealing sheen.

Fun Facts

The Ivory Coast produces almost half of the world's cocoa.

Cocoa butter is obtained during the chocolate manufacturing process and crystalizes in several different forms. To make chocolate, the prized beta crystals are selected because they have the highest melting point.

Cocoa butter is a natural remedy used especially for stretch marks.

Note: Exact measurements are crucial in soap making. Turn to page 21 for how-tos.

7.5 oz	mineral water	213 g
3 oz	lye (caustic soda)	85 g
1.5 lbs	extra virgin olive oil	682 g
3.5 oz	pure cocoa butter, grated	100 g
0.07 oz	vanilla essential oil	2 g

1. Wearing gloves and goggles, pour mineral water into a large saucepan. Add lye slowly, stirring gently until it is dissolved.

2. Using a thermometer, monitor the temperature of the lye mixture until it is between 120°F and 140°F (49°C and 60°C).

3. Meanwhile, in a separate saucepan, heat olive oil to between 120°F and 140°F (49°C and 60°C).

4. Remove olive oil from heat. Add lye mixture to olive oil, stirring slowly and trying not to splash.

5. Stir occasionally, every 15 minutes or so, until the mixture thickens and congeals. (It will have a texture similar to that of light mayonnaise.)

6. Stir in cocoa butter and essential oil. Stir for 1 minute with a spoon (or with a whisk, taking care not to create any foam).

7. Pour into a greased or paper-lined soap mold. Gently tap mold to remove any air bubbles.

8. Cover with a blanket or towel and let stand for 2 days. Uncover and let stand for an additional day if the mold is very large.

9. Turn soap out of mold. Wait another day, then cut into bars as desired.

10. Dry bars for 1 month, turning occasionally to ensure they are drying uniformly.

Cocoa Butter Soap's Action on the Skin

❧ This soap decongests the skin and gives it back its balance. It is highly recommended for people who have dry skin and those who are prone to getting cracks on their hands due to their line of work.

❧ Cocoa butter soap is very nourishing and moisturizing. It is beneficial to most types of skin, except for oily skin.

❧ While all soaps can be used on the face, this soap is especially well-suited for that purpose because of its gentleness. It is ideal for removing makeup; just keep in mind that it shouldn't get on the delicate skin of your eyelids.

GOAT'S MILK SOAP

Eternally Young Skin

Milk is a common food and has been consumed by humans since ancient times. The most frequently consumed types are cow's, goat's and sheep's milk. Cow's milk is directly consumed and is also used to make cheese and other dairy products. Sheep's and goat's milk are mainly used to make cheese. Goat's milk is often recommended if you have a milk allergy, because it contains less casein (a type of protein that can cause allergies in some people) than cow's milk.

People do consume other types of milk, including donkey's, mare's and buffalo's milk. The first two are rare and limited to very specific rural areas. Buffalo's milk is more widely used to make mozzarella cheese.

The Egyptians, Greeks and Romans knew that milk was beneficial to the skin, and some women of high society bathed in goat's or donkey's milk. It was said that they would keep their skin forever young that way. It's not necessary to go to such extremes, but it is true that milk baths are beneficial for the skin.

Lactic acid, which occurs naturally in milk, is also widely used in cosmetics. It produces considerable results when used to treat a variety of skin disorders.

The best kind of milk for cosmetics is, by far, donkey's milk. However, donkey's milk is very scarce—wild donkeys are endangered almost everywhere in the world.

Instead, this soap uses goat's milk (though we could use any other milk). Goat's milk contains lipoproteins that help transport nutrients into cells; it also gives the soap a soft, special texture.

Goat's Milk Soap

Tip

Goat's milk soap is appropriate for children, and people with sensitive skin and allergies.

• • •

Fun Fact

The fat molecules in goat's milk form smaller structures than those in other kinds of milk. Therefore, it does not form a thick cream layer, is more digestible and is a leading ingredient in cosmetics.

Note: Exact measurements are crucial in soap making. Turn to page 21 for how-tos.

7.5 oz	goat's milk (or cow's, sheep's or donkey's milk)	213 g
3 oz	lye (caustic soda)	85 g
1.5 lbs	extra virgin olive oil	682 g
0.35 oz	pure cocoa butter	10 g
0.18 oz	lemon essential oil	5 g

1. Wearing gloves and goggles, pour goat's milk into a large saucepan. Add lye slowly, stirring gently until it is dissolved.

2. Using a thermometer, monitor the temperature of the lye mixture until it is between 120°F and 140°F (49°C and 60°C).

3. Meanwhile, in a separate saucepan, heat olive oil to between 120°F and 140°F (49°C and 60°C).

4. Remove olive oil from heat. Add lye mixture to olive oil, stirring slowly and trying not to splash.

5. Stir occasionally, every 15 minutes or so, until the mixture thickens and congeals. (It will have a texture similar to that of light mayonnaise.)

6. Stir in cocoa butter and essential oil. Stir for 1 minute with a spoon (or with a whisk, taking care not to create any foam).

7. Pour into a greased or paper-lined soap mold. Gently tap mold to remove any air bubbles.

8. Cover with a blanket or towel and let stand for 2 days. Uncover and let stand for an additional day if the mold is very large.

9. Turn soap out of mold. Wait another day, then cut into bars as desired.

10. Dry bars for 1 month, turning occasionally to ensure they are drying uniformly.

Goat's Milk Soap's Action on the Skin

❧ Goat's milk soap is an emollient for sensitive skin, and is especially good for children and the elderly.

❧ Due to its gentleness, goat's milk soap is tolerated by any type of skin and is perfect for removing makeup.

❧ You can use the soap as a moisturizing mask by following these steps: moisten the skin, apply the soap, let it stand on the skin for a few minutes, and then rinse it off with water. You will quickly see how soft and smooth your skin becomes.

❧ If you want the soap to be more nutritious, add 2 tbsp (30 mL) cream along with the cocoa butter once the mixture has congealed.

CORN SOAP

Pearls of Sunshine for Your Skin

Corn (*Zea mays*) is a very nutritious grain that is high in mineral salts and vitamins A, B_1 (thiamin), B_2 (riboflavin), B_3 (niacin) and K.

It is native to America, where a number of different types grow. Its four main colors—white, yellow, black and red—are traditionally associated with the four cardinal directions. Corn varieties planted today are hybrids of the original varieties.

For soap making, we are interested in cornmeal. Look for cornmeal that is coarsely ground, because its main function will be to exfoliate the skin.

At the market, you will also find cornstarch-like flours, but these are of no use for soap making because they are completely refined and bleached. What you need is whole grain, stone-ground cornmeal, which is usually yellow and made from unpolished corn kernels. This is the only type that exfoliates the skin well.

If you can't find the right cornmeal, you can make your own. All you need is dried whole grain corn and a coffee grinder; a light grinding that does not turn the corn to powder is all that is required.

The soap incorporates lemon essential oil to enhance the cornmeal's exfoliating power and to help re-balance the skin.

If you like, you can use dried corn kernels instead of the cornmeal, in which case the soap will be good for massaging in circles over areas where fat accumulates.

Corn Soap

Fun Fact

The oldest known place where corn was grown is in Guatemala. The native people of that country continue grinding corn using stone mills; they use the resulting flour to make traditional tortillas, forming them by hand.

Note: Exact measurements are crucial in soap making. Turn to page 21 for how-tos.

7.5 oz	mineral water	213 g
3 oz	lye (caustic soda)	85 g
1.5 lbs	extra virgin olive oil	682 g
0.7 oz	coarse whole grain stone-ground cornmeal	20 g
0.18 oz	lemon essential oil	5 g

1. Wearing gloves and goggles, pour mineral water into a large saucepan. Add lye slowly, stirring gently until it is dissolved.

2. Using a thermometer, monitor the temperature of the lye mixture until it is between 120°F and 140°F (49°C and 60°C).

3. Meanwhile, in a separate saucepan, heat olive oil to between 120°F and 140°F (49°C and 60°C).

4. Remove olive oil from heat. Add lye mixture to olive oil, stirring slowly and trying not to splash.

5. Stir occasionally, every 15 minutes or so, until the mixture thickens and congeals. (It will have a texture similar to that of light mayonnaise.)

6. Stir in cornmeal and essential oil. Stir for 1 minute with a spoon (or with a whisk, taking care not to create foam).

7. Pour into a greased or paper-lined soap mold. Gently tap mold to remove any air bubbles.

8. Cover with a blanket or towel and let stand for 2 days. Uncover and let stand for an additional day if the mold is very large.

9. Turn soap out of mold. Wait another day, then cut into bars as desired.

10. Dry bars for 1 month, turning occasionally to ensure they are drying uniformly.

Corn Soap's Action on the Skin

❧ Use the soap as an exfoliant for the face and body. Massage it directly onto the skin, and be persistent around the knees and elbows to ensure good exfoliation.

❧ This is a very nutritious soap that works well on all skin types.

❧ If you make the whole corn kernel version, keep in mind that it is most useful on cellulite. Massage the soap directly over the skin using a circular motion.

❧ Corn soap is also good for massaging your feet to improve the entire body's circulation—but mainly the circulation in the legs. The massage should be administered from the heel to the tips of the toes, then back again, before continuing in a circular motion.

BRAN SOAP

Clean, Smooth and Soft

Bran is the outer husk of a grain once it has come loose from the kernel. It has long been a main ingredient in livestock feed. The best-known type is wheat bran, but there are many other kinds, including oat, barley, millet, rice and rye.

All brans have a similar nutritional function: to produce a dragging effect in the large intestine, helping the body eliminate waste. Consumed regularly, bran can help prevent constipation.

If you want a soap that cleanses deeply and purifies the skin, this is the one. It's even beneficial for hair because it respects the natural oils that shampoos tend to wash off.

For this soap, any bran will do. Oat and millet brans are softer; wheat and rye brans are a bit rougher. You can make this soap with a single type of bran or mix and match several different kinds, customizing the soap to your preference. Thanks to the bran, this soap is rich in vitamins and helps repair the skin.

If possible, buy organic bran, because insecticides and pesticides remain stuck to the grains' husks. This is not something that benefits the soap, much less your skin.

Bran Soap

This soap returns a natural glow to scaly skin. Suitable for oily areas, it regenerates and renews.

Tip

Wash your face with this soap, which is ideal for oily complexions.

• • •

Fun Fact

Japanese people call rice bran *nuka*. They fill cloth bags with it and rub them over their skin as they sit in saunas. They also make a soap out of rice bran, which is highly prized and rich in moisturizing polysaccharides.

Note: Exact measurements are crucial in soap making. Turn to page 21 for how-tos.

7.5 oz	mineral water	213 g
3 oz	lye (caustic soda)	85 g
1.5 lbs	extra virgin olive oil	682 g
0.35 oz	pure cocoa butter	10 g
1 tbsp	bran	15 mL
0.18 oz	orange essential oil	5 g

1. Wearing gloves and goggles, pour mineral water into a large saucepan. Add lye slowly, stirring gently until it is dissolved.

2. Using a thermometer, monitor the temperature of the lye mixture until it is between 120°F and 140°F (49°C and 60°C).

3. Meanwhile, in a separate saucepan, heat olive oil to between 120°F and 140°F (49°C and 60°C).

4. Remove olive oil from heat. Add lye mixture to olive oil, stirring slowly and trying not to splash.

5. Stir occasionally, every 15 minutes or so, until the mixture thickens and congeals. (It will have a texture similar to that of light mayonnaise.)

6. Stir in cocoa butter, bran and essential oil. Stir for 1 minute with a spoon (or with a whisk, taking care not to create foam).

7. Pour into a greased or paper-lined soap mold. Gently tap mold to remove any air bubbles.

8. Cover with a blanket or towel and let stand for 2 days. Uncover and let stand for an additional day if the mold is very large.

9. Turn soap out of mold. Wait another day, then cut into bars as desired.

10. Dry bars for 1 month, turning occasionally to ensure they are drying uniformly.

Bran Soap's Action on the Skin

- The purpose of this soap is to thoroughly cleanse and exfoliate the skin. It also provides it with significant vitamins and nutrients.

- It is suitable for all skin, at all ages.

- Bran soap especially benefits skin that is prematurely wrinkled, poorly maintained or exposed to extreme temperatures, as in climates that are very cold or very hot.

- This soap is ideal for use on hands, because it does not dry out the skin even when used repeatedly.

WHEAT GERM SOAP

The Source of Beauty

The germ of the wheat kernel (*Triticum* spp.) is the most nutritious part of the grain. Wheat is the most widespread grain throughout the world, because it is easy to grow; due to its high yield, it's more popular than rice.

Much of the bread eaten today is made with white flour, which has had the husk (or bran) and the germ removed. From a nutritional point of view, that means we eat denatured bread with few nutritious substances.

Wheat germ produces a dense oil that is very high in vitamin E, which is used to prepare numerous creams and cosmetics. The principal benefit of the oil is its great moisturizing and nutritive power, which is especially useful for minimizing the dreaded crow's feet that form around the eyes.

For this soap, you will need natural wheat germ oil, the most important known source of vitamin E. When buying the oil, keep several factors in mind. First, the oil should be virgin and come from the first cold pressing; second, it should be stored in a dark glass bottle to protect it from light exposure.

Wheat germ oil must be handled very carefully to preserve its vitamin E content. If the oil is extracted by means of high temperatures, a large amount of the vitamin is destroyed; if the oil is exposed to sunlight, the same thing occurs.

Wheat Germ Soap

Wheat germ is a natural source of vitamin E, which is also known as "the source of beauty."

Tip

Wheat germ soap is ideal for normal or combination skin. It's perfect to use for both your face and body.

• • •

Fun Fact

Wheat germ oil is rich in essential fatty acids, and it strengthens the immune system. It can also be used to make a hair mask that adds softness, vitality and elasticity.

Note: Exact measurements are crucial in soap making. Turn to page 21 for how-tos.

7.5 oz	mineral water	213 g
3 oz	lye (caustic soda)	85 g
1.5 lbs	extra virgin olive oil	682 g
0.35 oz	beeswax	10 g
1 tbsp	wheat germ	15 mL
0.7 oz	natural wheat germ oil	20 g

1. Wearing gloves and goggles, pour mineral water into a large saucepan. Add lye slowly, stirring gently until it is dissolved.

2. Using a thermometer, monitor the temperature of the lye mixture until it is between 120°F and 140°F (49°C and 60°C).

3. Meanwhile, in a separate saucepan, heat olive oil to between 120°F and 140°F (49°C and 60°C), stirring in beeswax slowly.

4. Remove olive oil mixture from heat. Add lye mixture to olive oil mixture, stirring slowly and trying not to splash.

5. Stir occasionally, every 15 minutes or so, until the mixture thickens and congeals. (It will have a texture similar to that of light mayonnaise.)

6. Stir in wheat germ and wheat germ oil. Stir for 1 minute with a spoon (or with a whisk, taking care not to create any foam).

7. Pour into a greased or paper-lined soap mold. Gently tap mold to remove any air bubbles.

8. Cover with a blanket or towel and let stand for 2 days. Uncover and let stand for an additional day if the mold is very large.

9. Turn soap out of mold. Wait another day, then cut into bars as desired.

10. Dry bars for 1 month, turning occasionally to ensure they are drying uniformly.

Wheat Germ Soap's Action on the Skin

- If you are looking for soap that prevents skin aging, this is the one. It moisturizes but does not produce oil. As it cleans, it also nourishes weak skin.

- Since this soap contains wheat germ, it will softly exfoliate if applied directly to the skin.

- Children's skin also benefits from this soap, as does the sensitive skin of the elderly.

- Keep wheat germ soap in mind for anyone who has dry or extra-dry skin.

BAY LEAF SOAP

The Soap of the East

The bay leaf (*Laurus nobilis*) comes from a tree that belongs to the Lauraceae family. It is widely cultivated throughout the Mediterranean Basin, where it originated.

The essential oil is obtained from the bay's smallest leaves and twigs. This oil is used to flavor various drinks and foods. In cosmetics, it is widely used in facial tonics, both for men and women. Essential oils are also made from the tree's berries, which healers have long used to treat sprains. Besides being an antiseptic, the bay leaf also battles the most common types of fungus, as well as eczema.

Ground bay leaves will work perfectly for this soap recipe. It is best if you grind them yourself. It's very simple: just put dried bay leaves in a clean coffee grinder and grind them until they are completely pulverized.

As is the case with all of the extra ingredients in the previous and following soaps, we have to remember something important: to always use organically grown products.

This recipe includes the essential oil that comes from the leaves and twigs of the bay tree. You can also add about 20 drops of lavender essential oil to the soap, if you like.

Bay Leaf Soap

Bay leaf soap is ideal for people who have oily and acne-prone skin.

Tip

This is an excellent hand soap, and it's the dream bar for any woman with sensitive skin.

• • •

Fun Fact

A mix of bay leaves, olive oil and alkaline ash made up the earliest soap, which was manufactured in Syria in biblical times to protect the skin of people who traveled to the desert. Today, bay leaf oil is used instead.

Note: Exact measurements are crucial in soap making. Turn to page 21 for how-tos.

7.5 oz	mineral water	213 g
3 oz	lye (caustic soda)	85 g
1.5 lbs	extra virgin olive oil	682 g
0.35 oz	beeswax	10 g
1 tbsp	ground bay leaves	15 mL
0.1 oz	bay leaf essential oil	3 g

1. Wearing gloves and goggles, pour mineral water into a large saucepan. Add lye slowly, stirring gently until it is dissolved.

2. Using a thermometer, monitor the temperature of the lye mixture until it is between 120°F and 140°F (49°C and 60°C).

3. Meanwhile, in a separate saucepan, heat olive oil to between 120°F and 140°F (49°C and 60°C), stirring in beeswax slowly.

4. Remove olive oil mixture from heat. Add lye mixture to olive oil mixture, stirring slowly and trying not to splash.

5. Stir occasionally, every 15 minutes or so, until the mixture thickens and congeals. (It will have a texture similar to that of light mayonnaise.)

6. Stir in ground bay leaves and essential oil. Stir for 1 minute with a spoon (or with a whisk, taking care not to create any foam).

7. Pour into a greased or paper-lined soap mold. Gently tap mold to remove any air bubbles.

8. Cover with a blanket or towel and let stand for 2 days. Uncover and let stand for an additional day if the mold is very large.

9. Turn soap out of mold. Wait another day, then cut into bars as desired.

10. Dry bars for 1 month, turning occasionally to ensure they are drying uniformly.

Bay Leaf Soap's Action on the Skin

❧ This is an antiseptic soap; in other words, it will protect the skin from potential infections. At the same time, it will also improve existing fungal or bacterial ailments.

❧ Bay leaf soap should be used by people who have oily, acne-prone skin. It is also good for combination skin, and even for sensitive skin; it cleanses while still safeguarding the skin's protective acid mantle.

❧ Bay leaf soap is excellent for hands. It's especially good for people who wash their hands frequently and helps protect their skin from drying out too much and cracking.

PROPOLIS SOAP

Life's Awakening

Propolis is a resinous compound that bees produce from a substance that they obtain from the buds and bark of some trees, such as cork, pine and oak. They use it to cover honeycomb panels, and it protects the hive and its residents from fungi, parasites and bacteria.

The substance, which is hard and brownish, acts as a natural fungicide and insecticide. Propolis has been used since the times of the Egyptians. When ingested, it has magnificent protective powers against colds, bronchitis and infections. More than 20 health-enhancing qualities of propolis have been recognized and tested, including antibiotic, antifungal, anti-inflammatory, analgesic, anesthetic and healing properties.

Propolis also helps form scar tissue. When used externally, it gives unsurpassable results fighting ulcers, hemorrhoids, burns and warts.

It can be found in capsule, powder and syrup form. For this soap, I recommend using the semi-liquid form. It comes in a dark glass jar, which ensures all of its properties are maintained.

Propolis contains 30% beeswax, but we will also add the amount of beeswax specified in the ingredient list to our soap. This formula is a bit special, precisely because of the presence of propolis.

After a few months, all soaps tend to dry out a bit, and they sometimes shrink—but they do not lose any of their virtues. However, propolis soap will stay as is for a few years, looking just like it did on the day it was made.

Propolis Soap

Propolis is one of nature's most valuable and exquisite products.

Fun Fact

Bees manufacture propolis from a substance found in tree buds; they cover the hive's walls with it in the winter to protect them from bacteria and fungi.

Note: Exact measurements are crucial in soap making. Turn to page 21 for how-tos.

7.5 oz	mineral water	213 g
3 oz	lye (caustic soda)	85 g
1.5 lbs	extra virgin olive oil	682 g
0.35 oz	beeswax	10 g
0.7 oz	propolis	20 g
0.15 oz	ylang-ylang essential oil	4 g

1. Wearing gloves and goggles, pour mineral water into a large saucepan. Add lye slowly, stirring gently until it is dissolved.

2. Using a thermometer, monitor the temperature of the lye mixture until it is between 120°F and 140°F (49°C and 60°C).

3. Meanwhile, in a separate saucepan, heat olive oil to between 120°F and 140°F (49°C and 60°C), stirring in beeswax slowly.

4. Remove olive oil mixture from heat. Add lye mixture to olive oil mixture, stirring slowly and trying not to splash.

5. Stir occasionally, every 15 minutes or so, until the mixture thickens and congeals. (It will have a texture similar to that of light mayonnaise.)

6. Stir in propolis and essential oil. Stir for 1 minute with a spoon (or with a whisk, taking care not to create foam).

7. Pour into a greased or paper-lined soap mold. Gently tap mold to remove any air bubbles.

8. Cover with a blanket or towel and let stand for 2 days. Uncover and let stand for an additional day if the mold is very large.

9. Turn soap out of mold. Wait another day, then cut into bars as desired.

10. Dry bars for 1 month, turning occasionally to ensure they are drying uniformly.

Propolis Soap's Action on the Skin

- This is the most complete soap, and the one that adapts best to any type of skin: sensitive, dry, oily and acne-prone skin alike will benefit from its nutritive and remineralizing properties.

- Propolis soap is also suitable for anyone who suffers from psoriasis.

- This is one of the most suitable soaps for baby skin, and it is just as beneficial for the elderly.

- As a makeup remover, propolis soap is excellent. Just make sure you don't apply it to the delicate skin of the lower eyelid.

ORANGE SOAP

Mediterranean Sighs

The orange (*Citrus sinensis*) is the fruit of a tree that belongs to the Rutaceae family. The variety we are concerned with comes from the sweet orange tree. This soap uses the zest, juice and essential oil of the sweet orange.

The juice for this recipe should be freshly squeezed natural orange juice. Don't use bottled juices, because many of them come from concentrate, and most have preservatives and artificial coloring. You don't want your soap to contain foreign substances that could ruin it.

Orange zest will serve as decoration. You can incorporate it according to your own personal preference: finely sliced with a knife or shredded with a grater to different thicknesses. A healthy zest without dark spots is desirable.

The essential oil should be 100% sweet orange. Synthetic oils used for incense burners have no place in this soap. Remember that only pure essential oils are authentic and natural.

As with other soaps, if you want to enjoy an intense orange scent, sprinkle a few drops of orange essential oil on the walls and lid of the box in which you store the hardened, dried pieces of soap. That way, you will intensify the soap's aroma, which slightly decreases after one month of drying.

Orange Soap

The scent of the orange, fresh and sweet, is a bonus that comes with its benefits for the skin. It makes the person using the soap happy, contributing optimism and cheeriness to the experience.

Fun Fact

Portuguese merchants first introduced the sweet orange to Europe in the 15th century, importing it from India. Sailors planted sweet orange trees along their routes to prevent scurvy.

Note: Exact measurements are crucial in soap making. Turn to page 21 for how-tos.

7.5 oz	orange juice	213 g
3 oz	lye (caustic soda)	85 g
1.5 lbs	extra virgin olive oil	682 g
0.35 oz	beeswax	10 g
	Zest of 1 orange, grated or sliced into small pieces	
0.35 oz	orange essential oil	10 g

1. Wearing gloves and goggles, pour orange juice into a large saucepan. Add lye slowly, stirring gently until it is dissolved.

2. Using a thermometer, monitor the temperature of the lye mixture until it is between 120°F and 140°F (49°C and 60°C).

3. Meanwhile, in a separate saucepan, heat olive oil to between 120°F and 140°F (49°C and 60°C), stirring in beeswax slowly.

4. Remove olive oil mixture from heat. Add lye mixture to olive oil mixture, stirring slowly and trying not to splash.

5. Stir occasionally, every 15 minutes or so, until the mixture thickens and congeals. (It will have a texture similar to that of light mayonnaise.)

6. Stir in orange zest and essential oil. Stir for 1 minute with a spoon (or with a whisk, taking care not to create foam).

7. Pour into a greased or paper-lined soap mold. Gently tap mold to remove any air bubbles.

8. Cover with a blanket or towel and let stand for 2 days. Uncover and let stand for an additional day if the mold is very large.

9. Turn soap out of mold. Wait another day, then cut into bars as desired.

10. Dry bars for 1 month, turning occasionally to ensure they are drying uniformly.

Orange Soap's Action on the Skin

- This soap is ideal for dull, weak or wrinkled skin, even if it is young. It is also effective on skin that tends to be oily.

- You can use this soap on the face and the body. Remember, though, that you need to moisturize the skin after using it—at least once a day (preferably before bedtime for the face).

- Because of the orange juice, this soap is high in vitamin C (also known as ascorbic acid).

- Some prestigious cosmetic brands have recently conducted studies and found that vitamin C has anti-aging benefits for the skin.

VANILLA SOAP

The Fragrance of the Tropics

Vanilla (*Vanilla planifolia*) belongs to the orchid family. It is native to the Americas but is currently grown throughout the tropics. This climbing plant is about 20 feet (6 meters) high and produces fruit in the form of elongated, fleshy pods full of tiny seeds. Once fermented and dried, the fruits become the brownish pods that we recognize as vanilla beans.

Vanilla is mainly used to flavor foods, such as ice cream, chocolate and dairy products. When the pod is drying, whitish crystals, called vanillin, form on the surface. Vanilla essential oil, extracted from vanilla pods, is part of many perfumes and colognes. Due to the complex process used to produce it, the oil is both prized and scarce.

Vanilla powder is sold in glass jars, and whole pods are sold in vacuum-packed packages. For this soap, I recommend using vanilla powder. Its small granules are easy to incorporate and offer an unmistakable scent.

If you like, you can decorate the soap with a whole vanilla pod once the block is formed in the mold.

If you find it impossible to get vanilla essential oil, you can add a small amount of the vanilla extract you normally use in cooking.

Vanilla Soap

Warm and sweet, subtle yet penetrating, vanilla makes us travel back in time. This soap's exquisite fragrance both soothes and brings harmony.

Fun Facts

The vanilla plant is an orchid with an intense scent. Its name comes from *vainilla*, the Spanish word for "sheath" because the fruit is shaped like a very small sheath. The name was given to the plant by Spanish explorers when they reached the Americas.

The scent of vanilla reminds us of mother's milk. The Aztecs considered vanilla an aphrodisiac.

Note: Exact measurements are crucial in soap making. Turn to page 21 for how-tos.

7.5 oz	mineral water	213 g
3 oz	lye (caustic soda)	85 g
1.5 lbs	extra virgin olive oil	682 g
0.35 oz	beeswax	10 g
0.18 oz	vanilla powder	5 g
0.04 oz	vanilla essential oil	1 g

1. Wearing gloves and goggles, pour mineral water into a large saucepan. Add lye slowly, stirring gently until it is dissolved.

2. Using a thermometer, monitor the temperature of the lye mixture until it is between 120°F and 140°F (49°C and 60°C).

3. Meanwhile, in a separate saucepan, heat olive oil to between 120°F and 140°F (49°C and 60°C), stirring in beeswax slowly.

4. Remove olive oil mixture from heat. Add lye mixture to olive oil mixture, stirring slowly and trying not to splash.

5. Stir occasionally, every 15 minutes or so, until the mixture thickens and congeals. (It will have a texture similar to that of light mayonnaise.)

6. Stir in vanilla powder and essential oil. Stir for 1 minute with a spoon (or with a whisk, taking care not to create any foam).

7. Pour into a greased or paper-lined soap mold. Gently tap mold to remove any air bubbles.

8. Cover with a blanket or towel and let stand for 2 days. Uncover and let stand for an additional day if the mold is very large.

9. Turn soap out of mold. Wait another day, then cut into bars as desired.

10. Dry bars for 1 month, turning occasionally to ensure they are drying uniformly.

Vanilla Soap's Action on the Skin

❧ The main function of this soap is to provide a fragrance that calms the senses, though it also has a relaxing effect on the skin itself.

❧ I recommend it for cleansing the skin after a soothing bath. An enveloping, tropical scent that enhances the pleasure of the bath will do anyone good.

❧ This soap is not recommended for people with sensitive skin, such as babies or the elderly.

CLAY SOAP

The Finest of Soils

Clay has been used since ancient times in a number of health treatments. There is a wide array of types of clay. Depending on the ailment being treated, white, green or red clay may be an ingredient, or a variety from a specific region or locality may be chosen.

Clay should be pure and collected at a certain depth in clean places that are far away from possible pollutants; not near busy highways, factories or hazardous spills.

The beneficial effect of clay on strains, sprains and inflammations has been proven. Clay is also used to treat osteoarthritis, rheumatism, atherosclerosis and bone pain. In cosmetics, different clays are used for different reasons. Clay facials that cleanse and degrease the skin are very effective. So are full-body treatments used to treat disorders such as cellulitis and poor circulation, and treatments that oxygenate the skin and cleanse it of impurities.

Some people even ingest clay in order to treat different internal disorders, but we are more concerned with its healing properties for the skin.

For this soap, you will use kaolin, a type of very pure white clay that is notable for its ability to cleanse and oxygenate the skin.

You can buy kaolin clay at specialty stores, herbalists' shops and even at some pharmacies. Make sure it is pure, without any kind of additives. An additional guarantee is if the clay is labeled as suitable for internal consumption—that means that the health checks are stricter than they are for clay used in cosmetics.

Clay Soap

Fun Fact

From kaolin to potter's mud, clay is the finest inorganic material in nature. When wet, it has plastic properties; when baked, it turns to ceramic.

Note: Exact measurements are crucial in soap making. Turn to page 21 for how-tos.

7.5 oz	mineral water	213 g
3 oz	lye (caustic soda)	85 g
1.5 lbs	extra virgin olive oil	682 g
1 tbsp	kaolin clay	15 mL
0.18 oz	rosemary essential oil	5 g

1. Wearing gloves and goggles, pour mineral water into a large saucepan. Add lye slowly, stirring gently until it is dissolved.

2. Using a thermometer, monitor the temperature of the lye mixture until it is between 120°F and 140°F (49°C and 60°C).

3. Meanwhile, in a separate saucepan, heat olive oil to between 120°F and 140°F (49°C and 60°C).

4. Remove olive oil from heat. Add lye mixture to olive oil, stirring slowly and trying not to splash.

5. Stir occasionally, every 15 minutes or so, until the mixture thickens and congeals. (It will have a texture similar to that of light mayonnaise.)

6. Stir in clay and essential oil. Stir for 1 minute with a spoon (or with a whisk, taking care not to create foam).

7. Pour into a greased or paper-lined soap mold. Gently tap mold to remove any air bubbles.

8. Cover with a blanket or towel and let stand for 2 days. Uncover and let stand for an additional day if the mold is very large.

9. Turn soap out of mold. Wait another day, then cut into bars as desired.

10. Dry bars for 1 month, turning occasionally to ensure they are drying uniformly.

Clay Soap's Action on the Skin

- This soap cleanses pores, and degreases and oxygenates skin, thus helping to maintain healthy skin that's free of impurities.

- Clay soap is good for all types of skin. However, keep in mind that clay soap should not be used every day on sensitive skin; a few days a week is tolerable, though. It is especially advisable to use this soap on acne-prone oily and combination skin. Oily skin needs to be cleaned more assiduously than dry skin.

- If you want the soap to be even more effective and gently exfoliate, apply it directly to the skin as a mask. Let it stand for a few minutes and then rinse it off with water.

OAT SOAP

Your Skin's Best Friend

The common oat (*Avena sativa*) is a grain from the Poaceae family, used mainly as food for people and animals. Oats are extremely nutritious, and many generations of children have grown up eating them. They are quite popular, especially in northern Europe, where they are mainly eaten at breakfast, flaked or in porridge.

It is interesting to note that oats are especially useful for feeding to racehorses. The grain provides slow-release carbohydrates, which provide vital fuel for the animals' enormous exertion.

In the world of cosmetics, the great virtues that oat extracts offer when used in skin-care products have caused a revolution in the past few years. This happened once it was demonstrated that oats have exceptional properties that help people with sensitive skin, especially children and the elderly.

For this soap, you can use any variety of oats, because all—and there are many types—are good. What is important is that they are organically grown. Remember that the husks of grains are where all insecticide and pesticide residues remain. These residues should not end up in your soap.

Cocoa butter is also included in this recipe. It lends the soap even greater silkiness and especially excellent moisturizing capabilities. Lemon essential oil gives the bars a soft fragrance.

Oat Soap

This soap is renowned because it preserves the skin's natural moisture.

Tips

Use organic oats for this recipe.

To make the oat infusion, in a bowl, pour 7.5 oz (213 g) boiling water over 1 tbsp (15 mL) rolled oats. Cover and let stand for 5 minutes. Strain and weigh for recipe.

• • •

Fun Facts

Oats have been grown in Europe since the Bronze Age. They are better adapted to humid climates and acidic soils than wheat is.

This soap decreases the hardness of water with high limestone content.

Note: Exact measurements are crucial in soap making. Turn to page 21 for how-tos.

7.5 oz	oat infusion (see tips, at left)	213 g
3 oz	lye (caustic soda)	85 g
1.5 lbs	extra virgin olive oil	682 g
0.35 oz	pure cocoa butter	10 g
1 tbsp	rolled oats or whole grain oat flour	15 mL
0.07 oz	lemon essential oil	2 g

1. Wearing gloves and goggles, pour oat infusion into a large saucepan. Add lye slowly, stirring gently until it is dissolved.

2. Using a thermometer, monitor the temperature of the lye mixture until it is between 120°F and 140°F (49°C and 60°C).

3. Meanwhile, in a separate saucepan, heat olive oil to between 120°F and 140°F (49°C and 60°C).

4. Remove olive oil from heat. Add lye mixture to olive oil, stirring slowly and trying not to splash.

5. Stir occasionally, every 15 minutes or so, until the mixture thickens and congeals. (It will have a texture similar to that of light mayonnaise.)

6. Stir in cocoa butter, rolled oats and essential oil. Stir for 1 minute with a spoon (or with a whisk, taking care not to create foam).

7. Pour into a greased or paper-lined soap mold. Gently tap mold to remove any air bubbles.

8. Cover with a blanket or towel and let stand for 2 days. Uncover and let stand for an additional day if the mold is very large.

9. Turn soap out of mold. Wait another day, then cut into bars as desired.

10. Dry bars for 1 month, turning occasionally to ensure they are drying uniformly.

Oat Soap's Action on the Skin

- ❧ Oat soap is gentle to the skin's acid mantle, which protects it, and possesses great moisturizing power. The soap also provides the skin with many essential nutrients.

- ❧ It is ideal for all types of skin, especially for children and people with sensitive skin.

- ❧ Oat soap is highly recommended as a makeup remover. Just remember to avoid the eye area.

- ❧ This soap will have the same benefits for the skin whether it is made with rolled oats or oat flour. The only difference is that soap made with rolled oats can be used for gentle exfoliation.

MUNG BEAN SOAP

A Breath of Life for the Skin

Of all the properties of the mung bean *(Vigna radiata)*—which are many—the most important is its richness in protein. This is the legume with the highest protein content after the soybean, which therefore makes it a major protein source in vegetarian diets.

The mung bean is often confused with the soybean, and some people mistakenly call it the green soybean. It is noted for its wealth of minerals, especially magnesium. It is also high in folic acid and all of the B vitamins.

Native to India, the mung bean was so virtuous that news of it reached China, where people began eating it in sprout form 3,000 years ago.

This soap is designed to help get rid of fatty deposits located in different areas of the body. The soap also uses fucus seaweed, which releases a substance that helps eliminate water retained in the tissues.

When you buy mung beans, make sure they are smooth-skinned. You can also use red adzuki beans *(Vigna angularis),* but add a generous amount to ensure the bars will give a good massage.

Cellulite is produced by a variety of factors, including poor circulation in the affected area. Marjoram essential oil helps circulation become more fluid. If you prefer, you can substitute lemon, lemongrass or coriander essential oil.

Mung Bean Soap

This soap renews and nourishes skin like no other.

Tips

The mung beans embedded in the soap give an exceptional, invigorating massage to tired legs.

To make the fucus seaweed infusion, in a bowl, pour 7.5 oz (213 g) boiling water over 2 tbsp (30 mL) dried fucus seaweed. Cover and let stand for 5 minutes. Strain and weigh for recipe.

• • •

Fun Fact

Mung beans provide no less than 25 grams of protein in one 3.5-oz (100 gram) serving. The best way to eat them is in sprout form in salads, but the beans themselves are delicious simmered as well.

Note: Exact measurements are crucial in soap making. Turn to page 21 for how-tos.

7.5 oz	fucus seaweed infusion (see tips, at left)	213 g
3 oz	lye (caustic soda)	85 g
1.5 lbs	extra virgin olive oil	682 g
0.35 oz	beeswax	10 g
6 tbsp	dried mung beans	90 mL
1 tbsp	granulated sugar	15 mL
0.18 oz	marjoram essential oil	5 g

1. Wearing gloves and goggles, pour fucus infusion into a large saucepan. Add lye slowly, stirring gently until it is dissolved.

2. Using a thermometer, monitor the temperature of the lye mixture until it is between 120°F and 140°F (49°C and 60°C).

3. Meanwhile, in a separate saucepan, heat olive oil to between 120°F and 140°F (49°C and 60°C), stirring in beeswax slowly.

4. Remove olive oil mixture from heat. Add lye mixture to olive oil mixture, stirring slowly and trying not to splash.

5. Stir occasionally, every 15 minutes or so, until the mixture thickens and congeals. (It will have a texture similar to that of light mayonnaise.)

6. Stir in mung beans, sugar and essential oil. Stir for 1 minute with a spoon (or with a whisk, taking care not to create foam).

7. Pour into a greased or paper-lined soap mold. Gently tap mold to remove any air bubbles.

8. Cover with a blanket or towel and let stand for 2 days. Uncover and let stand for an additional day if the mold is very large.

9. Turn soap out of mold. Wait another day, then cut into bars as desired.

10. Dry bars for 1 month, turning occasionally to dry uniformly.

Mung Bean Soap's Action on the Skin

- Use this soap on areas where water retention or cellulitis is a problem. Be consistent to ensure a satisfactory result.

- Massage the soap over affected areas of the legs, buttocks, arms or abdomen daily using a circular motion.

- If you want to reinforce the soap's effect, apply anti-cellulite cream after the massage.

- Massages with this soap work better in the shower. First, get your whole body wet, then perform the massage.

GREEN TEA SOAP

The Best Antioxidant

Green tea, whose health-enhancing properties are known worldwide, is made from the leaves of a shrub with the Latin name *Camellia sinensis*.

In some Asian countries, including China and Japan, green tea is part of daily life and the basis of ancient customs. For these cultures, preparing tea is an age-old ritual, in which every little action is done in a specific manner while taking time to reflect.

Japanese and Chinese women suffer less from cellulite than Western women, and while this can be explained by the variations in diet alone, what may make the real difference is that they drink larger quantities of green tea. The incidence of cancer is also significantly lower in Japan and China than in the West, because green tea is a powerful anticancer agent. It is also purifying and a great antioxidant.

When ingested, green tea has a purifying effect. When infusions are applied externally, they repair and moisturize the skin. At present, there are innumerable green tea–based cosmetics: creams, body lotions, bath gels, shampoos and more.

You will use natural green tea (whole dried leaves) to make the infusion for your soap. For an extra ingredient, you will tear open a bag of conventional green tea and add its contents to the soap mixture after it has congealed.

Green Tea Soap

Green tea is excellent at soothing skin and prevents aging.

Tips

When it comes to the best variety of green tea for cosmetic use, I recommend the Gunpowder variety.

To make the green tea infusion, in a bowl, pour 7.5 oz (213 g) boiling water over 2 tbsp (30 mL) natural green tea. Cover and let stand for 5 minutes. Strain and weigh for recipe.

• • •

Fun Fact

After water, green tea is the most-consumed beverage around the world. In Japan, the infusion may be accompanied by garden flowers, such as cherry or lotus blossoms, to increase relaxation.

Note: Exact measurements are crucial in soap making. Turn to page 21 for how-tos.

7.5 oz	green tea infusion (see tips, at left)	213 g
3 oz	lye (caustic soda)	85 g
1.5 lbs	extra virgin olive oil	682 g
0.35 oz	pure cocoa butter	10 g
1	small bag green tea, torn open	1
0.07 oz	mint essential oil	2 g

1. Wearing gloves and goggles, pour green tea infusion into a large saucepan. Add lye slowly, stirring gently until it is dissolved.

2. Using a thermometer, monitor the temperature of the lye mixture until it is between 120°F and 140°F (49°C and 60°C).

3. Meanwhile, in a separate saucepan, heat olive oil to between 120°F and 140°F (49°C and 60°C).

4. Remove olive oil from heat. Add lye mixture to olive oil, stirring slowly and trying not to splash.

5. Stir occasionally, every 15 minutes or so, until the mixture thickens and congeals. (It will have a texture similar to that of light mayonnaise.)

6. Stir in cocoa butter, contents of green tea bag and essential oil. Stir for 1 minute with a spoon (or with a whisk, taking care not to create foam).

7. Pour into a greased or paper-lined soap mold. Gently tap mold to remove any air bubbles.

8. Cover with a blanket or towel and let stand for 2 days. Uncover and let stand for an additional day if the mold is very large.

9. Turn soap out of mold. Wait another day, then cut into bars as desired.

10. Dry bars for 1 month, turning occasionally to ensure they are drying uniformly.

Green Tea Soap's Action on the Skin

- This soap purifies, moisturizes and repairs skin.

- It soothes irritated tissues and skin damage caused by extreme temperatures, both high and low.

- All types of skin—whether dry, oily, dehydrated or sensitive—can benefit from the use of this soap.

- Due to its gentle nature, green tea soap is also suitable as a hand soap because it can be used frequently.

CEDAR SOAP

The Most Fragrant Soap

There are four varieties of cedar (*Cedrus* spp.): those from Lebanon, from the Atlas Mountains in North Africa, from Cyprus and from the Himalayas. The most prized is the Lebanese variety (*Cedrus libani*), but it has been exploited for so many years that there are hardly any specimens left in Turkey and Lebanon.

The essential oil, which is used for meditation and is very helpful in caring for dry skin, is obtained from cedar wood. The oils you will find on the market come from cedar trees grown in the Atlas Mountains and the Himalayas, which have a very high concentration of oil.

The Egyptians used cedar essential oil in embalming and as an insect repellent. Its positive effects in treating respiratory ailments were also known. The oil was already used in that period for perfume, especially for men; cedar's masculine aroma also blends well with other scents.

In cosmetics, cedar essential oil is used to produce creams, toners and soaps. The cleaning product industry uses it in detergents, cleansers and air fresheners.

For this soap, you may use whichever variety is easiest to obtain. All of the essential oils have similar properties.

The infusion should be made using dry cedar wood chips, whose intense aroma will surprise you. If possible, the wood chips and the essential oil you choose should come from the same variety of cedar tree. It is not difficult to find both in specialty and herbalists' shops.

Cedar Soap

Besides nourishing the skin, cedar soap also stimulates and invigorates the body and spirit.

Tips

Cedar soap keeps the skin nice and smooth if used regularly.

To make the cedar infusion, in a bowl, pour 7.5 oz (213 g) boiling water over 1 tbsp (15 mL) cedar chips. Cover and let stand for 5 minutes. Strain and weigh for recipe.

• • •

Fun Facts

Cedar is the most-referenced tree in the Bible; it was used in Egypt and in the first Temple of Jerusalem because the scent of its wood wards off insects and worms.

Atlas Mountain cedar is an antiseptic.

Note: Exact measurements are crucial in soap making. Turn to page 21 for how-tos.

7.5 oz	cedar infusion (see tips, at left)	213 g
3 oz	lye (caustic soda)	85 g
1.5 lbs	extra virgin olive oil	682 g
0.35 oz	beeswax	10 g
0.35 oz	cedar essential oil	10 g

1. Wearing gloves and goggles, pour cedar infusion into a large saucepan. Add lye slowly, stirring gently until it is dissolved.

2. Using a thermometer, monitor the temperature of the lye mixture until it is between 120°F and 140°F (49°C and 60°C).

3. Meanwhile, in a separate saucepan, heat olive oil to between 120°F and 140°F (49°C and 60°C), stirring in beeswax slowly.

4. Remove olive oil mixture from heat. Add lye mixture to olive oil mixture, stirring slowly and trying not to splash.

5. Stir occasionally, every 15 minutes or so, until the mixture thickens and congeals. (It will have a texture similar to that of light mayonnaise.)

6. Stir in essential oil. Stir for 1 minute with a spoon (or with a whisk, taking care not to create foam).

7. Pour into a greased or paper-lined soap mold. Gently tap mold to remove any air bubbles.

8. Cover with a blanket or towel and let stand for 2 days. Uncover and let stand for an additional day if the mold is very large.

9. Turn soap out of mold. Wait another day, then cut into bars as desired.

10. Dry bars for 1 month, turning occasionally to ensure they are drying uniformly.

Cedar Soap's Action on the Skin

- Cedar soap is good for a wide range of conditions; it acts positively to treat dermatitis, eczema, oily skin and acne alike.

- This soap is perfect for all types of skin, whether it has problems or not. If you are lucky enough to have healthy skin, it will only serve to cleanse; if you have a skin ailment, it will solve the problem in addition to cleansing.

- The scent of cedar is very masculine but is subtle in this soap, so women will also enjoy using it.

TEA TREE SOAP

The Scent that Heals

The tea tree (*Melaleuca alternifolia*) belongs to the Myrtacaeae family. It grows only in Australia, where it is known as the melaleuca, or paperbark, tree. It has a scent similar to that of eucalyptus. It has nothing to do with tea; it was given that name because the Australian Aborigines drank infusions made from the leaves in order benefit from the tree's properties.

An unparalleled essential oil is extracted from the tree's leaves and twigs. This oil fights effectively against viruses, bacteria and fungi. No other oil compares to this one in terms of the number of ailments it can mitigate.

A drop of tea tree essential oil beneath the tongue cures a cough rapidly and wards off colds and bronchitis.

Babies often suffer from diaper rash, a localized skin irritation of the area that comes into contact with the diaper, caused by exposure to urine and feces. Oftentimes, even if a baby is cleaned regularly, he or she will still exhibit this irritation, and it will not disappear until a diaper is no longer used. A practically infallible remedy is to mix 1 tsp (5 mL) almond oil with two drops of tea tree essential oil and apply it to the irritated area when the diaper is changed. Once the irritation subsides, only almond oil needs to be applied.

For this soap, you will need tea tree leaves to make the infusion and pure tea tree essential oil as an extra ingredient. Look for both at specialty and herbalists' shops. Enjoy the aroma of this prodigious aromatic cure-all, which is one of the best natural antiseptics.

Tea Tree Soap

The tea tree creates an essence that softens, protects and soothes.

Tip

To make the tea tree leaf infusion, in a bowl, pour 7.5 oz (213 g) boiling water over 2 tbsp (30 mL) tea tree leaves. Cover and let stand for 5 minutes. Strain and weigh for recipe.

• • •

Fun Facts

The tea tree is a shrub that grows naturally along the subtropical coast of Australia (a similar shrub grows in New Zealand) in humid and swampy areas. It has a black trunk and whitish branches.

The essential oil is colorless. It is distilled from leaves and tender branches and is cool and pleasant.

Note: Exact measurements are crucial in soap making. Turn to page 21 for how-tos.

7.5 oz	tea tree leaf infusion (see tip, at left)	213 g
3 oz	lye (caustic soda)	85 g
1.5 lbs	extra virgin olive oil	682 g
0.35 oz	beeswax	10 g
0.35 oz	tea tree essential oil	10 g
1 tsp	poppy seeds, for garnish	5 mL

1. Wearing gloves and goggles, pour tea tree leaf infusion into a large saucepan. Add lye slowly, stirring gently until it is dissolved.

2. Using a thermometer, monitor the temperature of the lye mixture until it is between 120°F and 140°F (49°C and 60°C).

3. Meanwhile, in a separate saucepan, heat olive oil to between 120°F and 140°F (49°C and 60°C), stirring in beeswax slowly.

4. Remove olive oil mixture from heat. Add lye mixture to olive oil mixture, stirring slowly and trying not to splash.

5. Stir occasionally, every 15 minutes or so, until the mixture thickens and congeals. (It will have a texture similar to that of light mayonnaise.)

6. Stir in essential oil. Stir for 1 minute with a spoon (or with a whisk, taking care not to create foam).

7. Pour into a greased or paper-lined soap mold. Gently tap mold to remove any air bubbles. Sprinkle top of soap mixture with poppy seeds.

8. Cover with a blanket or towel and let stand for 2 days. Uncover and let stand for an additional day if the mold is very large.

9. Turn soap out of mold. Wait another day, then cut into bars as desired.

10. Dry bars for 1 month, turning occasionally to ensure they are drying uniformly.

Tea Tree Soap's Action on the Skin

- ❧ Tea tree soap is effective against acne, blisters, herpes, insect bites, diaper rash, infected wounds, athlete's foot and many more conditions.

- ❧ This soap can be used by almost anyone. It doesn't matter whether you have a skin problem, or dry or oily skin. It does everyone good.

- ❧ The only downside is that some people have an allergy to this tree, but that can happen with any soap. Avoid using soap made with plants that give you an allergic reaction.

AFTER EIGHT SOAP

A Treat for the Skin

This soap was inspired by the famous English mint chocolate candy of the same name. In addition to its healing properties, it is also a gift to the senses. This soap is a real treat when you shower or bathe and can enjoy its unmistakable aroma.

Cocoa is purifying and nutritious for the skin, and its effectiveness against cellulite and fat deposits has been proven. Peppermint is very good at fighting acne and excess fat, and its relaxing scent relieves headaches and migraines.

These two ingredients together are a good combination, both for the skin and for the senses, which are important, too.

Use 100% pure cocoa powder for this soap; the same type you would use to bake with. Cocoa butter, which is also important in this recipe, should be the pure form.

The variety of mint I recommend for this soap is peppermint (*Mentha piperita),* but spearmint (*Mentha spicata)* has similar properties and smells just as nice.

After selecting the variety of mint, you will need 1 tbsp (15 mL) fresh mint leaves to make the infusion and about 10 more leaves, chopped finely, to add to the soap as an extra ingredient.

After Eight Soap

This soap smells so good. You can't eat it, of course, but your whole body will have a delicious fragrance when you use it.

This soap smells so good. You can't eat it, of course, but your whole body will have a delicious fragrance when you use it.

Tip

To make the peppermint infusion, in a bowl, pour 7.5 oz (213 g) boiling water over 1 tbsp (15 mL) fresh peppermint leaves. Cover and let stand for 5 minutes. Strain and weigh for recipe.

• • •

Fun Fact

After Eight wafers are described as "mint enveloped in chocolate." They went into production in 1962 and, since 1988, their sole manufacturer has been Nestlé, which began adding cream to the recipe in 2007.

Note: Exact measurements are crucial in soap making. Turn to page 21 for how-tos.

7.5 oz	peppermint infusion (see tip, at left)	213 g
3 oz	lye (caustic soda)	85 g
1.5 lbs	extra virgin olive oil	682 g
0.7 oz	pure cocoa butter	20 g
1 tbsp	pure cocoa powder	15 mL
10	fresh peppermint leaves, finely chopped	10
0.35 oz	peppermint essential oil	10 g

1. Wearing gloves and goggles, pour peppermint infusion into a large saucepan. Add lye slowly, stirring gently until it is dissolved.

2. Using a thermometer, monitor the temperature of the lye mixture until it is between 120°F and 140°F (49°C and 60°C).

3. Meanwhile, in a separate saucepan, heat olive oil to between 120°F and 140°F (49°C and 60°C).

4. Remove olive oil from heat. Add lye mixture to olive oil, stirring slowly and trying not to splash.

5. Stir occasionally, every 15 minutes or so, until the mixture thickens and congeals. (It will have a texture similar to that of light mayonnaise.)

6. Stir in cocoa butter, cocoa powder, chopped peppermint and essential oil. Stir for 1 minute with a spoon (or with a whisk, taking care not to create foam).

7. Pour into a greased or paper-lined soap mold. Gently tap mold to remove any air bubbles.

8. Cover with a blanket or towel and let stand for 2 days. Uncover and let stand for an additional day if the mold is very large.

9. Turn soap out of mold. Wait another day, then cut into bars as desired.

10. Dry bars for 1 month, turning occasionally to dry uniformly.

After Eight Soap's Action on the Skin

❧ This soap is purifying, nutritious and very relaxing for the skin all over the body.

❧ After Eight soap is recommended for anyone suffering from acne and excess oil production.

❧ It is ideal for skin that, due to diet, has a strong odor, because it leaves behind a very pleasant fragrance.

❧ This soap also helps fight cellulite in areas where fat accumulates.

DEAD SEA SALT SOAP

Ancient Emanations

The Dead Sea is an inland sea with barely any inflowing freshwater, other than the trickle of the Jordan River. Because of that and the area's hot temperatures, its water has the highest concentration of salt in the world: 10 times more than any open sea, or between 12 and 13 oz per quart (350 and 370 g per liter). This salt, once extracted via evaporation, has curative qualities that have been exploited for millennia.

For this recipe, you will only need about 0.7 oz (20 g) of Dead Sea salt, which you can purchase at an herbalist's shop.

This salt's main characteristic is that it contains 21 minerals, including calcium, magnesium, bromine, potassium and others not found in other seas. It re-mineralizes the skin and lends it elements that make it healthier. The salt comes in various types and exhibits different colors and textures. There are grayish or brownish salts, and their texture depends on whether they have been crushed or left in natural crystal form. I recommend using the finely crushed variety for this soap.

Don't settle for imitations; only salts from the Dead Sea are authentic and especially rich in sodium, magnesium, potassium and iodine. King Herod and Cleopatra, in their day, came to anoint themselves with black mud from the sea's shallow banks and float while gazing at the sky. The salt crystallizes as the water at the shore recedes, and the minerals stay behind trapped in a haze of light-catching geometric shapes that will very soon become part of your favorite soap.

Dead Sea Salt Soap

Fun Facts

The salinity of the Dead Sea is 10 times higher than that of other seas. The concentration of salt means that people are especially buoyant, so it is impossible to immerse yourself in its medicinal waters. These waters have receded significantly due to economic activity in the region.

The salts in the water crystallize in the form of rocks, creating a ghostly landscape on the shores of the Dead Sea.

Note: Exact measurements are crucial in soap making. Turn to page 21 for how-tos.

7.5 oz	mineral water	213 g
3 oz	lye (caustic soda)	85 g
1.5 lbs	extra virgin olive oil	682 g
0.35 oz	pure cocoa butter	10 g
1 tbsp	fine Dead Sea salt	15 mL
0.1 oz	rosemary essential oil	3 g

1. Wearing gloves and goggles, pour mineral water into a large saucepan. Add lye slowly, stirring gently until it is dissolved.

2. Using a thermometer, monitor the temperature of the lye mixture until it is between 120°F and 140°F (49°C and 60°C).

3. Meanwhile, in a separate saucepan, heat olive oil to between 120°F and 140°F (49°C and 60°C).

4. Remove olive oil from heat. Add lye mixture to olive oil, stirring slowly and trying not to splash.

5. Stir occasionally, every 15 minutes or so, until the mixture thickens and congeals. (It will have a texture similar to that of light mayonnaise.)

6. Stir in cocoa butter, Dead Sea salt and essential oil. Stir for 1 minute with a spoon (or with a whisk, taking care not to create foam).

7. Pour into a greased or paper-lined soap mold. Gently tap mold to remove any air bubbles.

8. Cover with a blanket or towel and let stand for 2 days. Uncover and let stand for an additional day if the mold is very large.

9. Turn soap out of mold. Wait another day, then cut into bars as desired.

10. Dry bars for 1 month, turning occasionally to ensure they are drying uniformly.

Dead Sea Salt Soap's Action on the Skin

❧ This soap is ideal for use on dull, malnourished and dehydrated skin. It's also good for refreshing skin that has thickened with layers of dead cells due to lack of exfoliation.

❧ The function of Dead Sea salt soap is to remineralize the skin deeply and give it all the nutrients it needs.

❧ Once a week, let this soap stand on the skin for a few minutes, then rinse it off with water.

❧ I do not recommend this soap for babies' skin, which is sensitive.

BEACH SAND SOAP

Being Reborn

This soap has a very particular history. Like many discoveries, the reason behind it is one of the most interesting aspects.

My feet, like most women's, have a fine layer of skin that suffers the consequences of being exposed to the open air, being shod in sandals or flip-flops, or going around barefoot. During the winter, in forced isolation, my feet are kept in perfect condition, and they are as smooth as a baby's bottom. Tragedy strikes in the summer, because the joyous freedom from socks and shoes is paired with a series of undesirable side effects: my feet experience dryness, little cracks, roughness and the sensation of not having been cared for—ever.

But then something wonderful happened to me one summer: I was sitting on the beach playing with my daughters and we were trying to dig a big hole. I decided to dig it with my heels, and I made a big hole—yes, I did. When I got home and showered, I was astonished to find, while I was moisturizing my skin, that my feet were softer than ever. I remembered the wet sand that afternoon, and eureka! That was the reason my feet were so splendid.

Later, I continued researching and reached the conclusion that olive oil soap made with beach sand is the best exfoliant for the skin—that is, on the rough parts of the body. I can assure you that neither pumice nor any other concoction will create such a good, effective and gentle result.

The sand you add to this soap should be dry and clean. It's best to add clear, fine sand—and that type abounds in many places. Gather it in a clean area, then wash it with mineral water and leave it to dry in the sun. When it is completely dry, it is ready to use.

Beach Sand Soap

Return the softness of a newborn baby's skin to your body.

Tip

Use yellow sand that doesn't contain little black dots of mica, which will remain on the skin.

• • •

Fun Fact

The nature of beach sand varies depending on its origin. In Costa Rica, there are black volcanic sand beaches that suddenly turn yellow, while on nearby islands, the beaches are white.

Note: Exact measurements are crucial in soap making. Turn to page 21 for how-tos.

7.5 oz	mineral water	213 g
3 oz	lye (caustic soda)	85 g
1.5 lbs	extra virgin olive oil	682 g
0.4 oz	beeswax	12 g
2 tbsp	beach sand	30 mL
1 tbsp	fine natural sea salt	15 mL
0.15 oz	tea tree essential oil	4 g

1. Wearing gloves and goggles, pour mineral water into a large saucepan. Add lye slowly, stirring gently until it is dissolved.

2. Using a thermometer, monitor the temperature of the lye mixture until it is between 120°F and 140°F (49°C and 60°C).

3. Meanwhile, in a separate saucepan, heat olive oil to between 120°F and 140°F (49°C and 60°C), stirring in beeswax slowly.

4. Remove olive oil mixture from heat. Add lye mixture to olive oil mixture, stirring slowly and trying not to splash.

5. Stir occasionally, every 15 minutes or so, until the mixture thickens and congeals. (It will have a texture similar to that of light mayonnaise.)

6. Stir in sand, salt and essential oil. Stir for 1 minute with a spoon (or with a whisk, taking care not to create foam).

7. Pour into a greased or paper-lined soap mold. Gently tap mold to remove any air bubbles.

8. Cover with a blanket or towel and let stand for 2 days. Uncover and let stand for an additional day if the mold is very large.

9. Turn soap out of mold. Wait another day, then cut into bars as desired.

10. Dry bars for 1 month, turning occasionally to ensure they are drying uniformly.

Beach Sand Soap's Action on the Skin

- This soap is recommended for any area of the body where the skin is noticeably hard and rough.

- It can be used on the knees, elbows, heels and the entire foot.

- Use this soap to give a massage to each and every part of the foot. It will relax the legs and remove unsightly hard patches from the feet.

- Best of all, beach sand soap prevents discomfort from dry, cracked feet when walking.

ALOE VERA SOAP

The Bitter Substance

Aloe vera (*Aloe vera*) is a succulent plant of the Xanthorrhoeaceae family, which grows in the deserts of southern Africa.

Aloin is extracted by squeezing the plant's spiked cactus-type leaves. This greenish-yellow liquid is used to induce vomiting and should not be consumed. However, it has extraordinary virtues if used topically on the skin. For this soap, you will only need 1 to 2 tbsp (15 to 30 mL).

Aloe can be used as an energy food, but in that case the dermis and epidermis of the leaves must be discarded (they contain the bulk of the aloin and other irritating substances) and the pulp must be washed carefully. For soap, the opposite is true. If we want the aloe to yield its therapeutic properties, its juices must contain aloin. Simply squeeze the leaves to extract the juice.

Aloe vera has so many healthy properties that it is almost impossible to list them all: it is anti-infective, anti-inflammatory and soothing on cuts and burns; it promotes healing; it regenerates the skin; and it soothes and heals wounds, bruises, muscle or joint pain, acne, skin blemishes and so on.

The word *aloe* comes from Arabic and means "shining bitter substance," while the word *vera* is Latin for "true." The Egyptians and Sumerians used it in their day, and now there are many varieties grown in places far and wide.

Aloe Vera Soap

Tip

An aloe plant is easy to take care of, and all you need to do is snip one leaf in order to obtain the medicinal juice.

• • •

Fun Fact

Aloe vera has been used for 5,000 years by African healers. Each leaf has 75 nutritious elements, 20 minerals and 12 vitamins, in addition to another 200 components.

Note: Exact measurements are crucial in soap making. Turn to page 21 for how-tos.

7.5 oz	mineral water	213 g
3 oz	lye (caustic soda)	85 g
1.5 lbs	extra virgin olive oil	682 g
0.4 oz	beeswax	12 g
1.8 oz	aloe vera juice	50 g
0.18 oz	mint essential oil	5 g

1. Wearing gloves and goggles, pour mineral water into a large saucepan. Add lye slowly, stirring gently until it is dissolved.

2. Using a thermometer, monitor the temperature of the lye mixture until it is between 120°F and 140°F (49°C and 60°C).

3. Meanwhile, in a separate saucepan, heat olive oil to between 120°F and 140°F (49°C and 60°C), stirring in beeswax slowly.

4. Remove olive oil mixture from heat. Add lye mixture to olive oil mixture, stirring slowly and trying not to splash.

5. Stir occasionally, every 15 minutes or so, until the mixture thickens and congeals. (It will have a texture similar to that of light mayonnaise.)

6. Stir in aloe vera juice and essential oil. Stir for 1 minute with a spoon (or with a whisk, taking care not to create any foam).

7. Pour into a greased or paper-lined soap mold. Gently tap mold to remove any air bubbles.

8. Cover with a blanket or towel and let stand for 2 days. Uncover and let stand for an additional day if the mold is very large.

9. Turn soap out of mold. Wait another day, then cut into bars as desired.

10. Dry bars for 1 month, turning occasionally to ensure they are drying uniformly.

Aloe Vera Soap's Action on the Skin

- Aloe vera soap is very effective at treating burns, wounds and acne. It is soothing and moisturizing, and it stimulates the growth of cells and tissues. This is due to its steroid, enzyme and amino acid content. It stimulates the immune system, and contains anthraquinones, which generate soothing substances.

- Be aware that some people are allergic to aloe, and it causes them irritation. Test the soap on a small area of skin first.

- This soap is not recommended for children under six years of age.

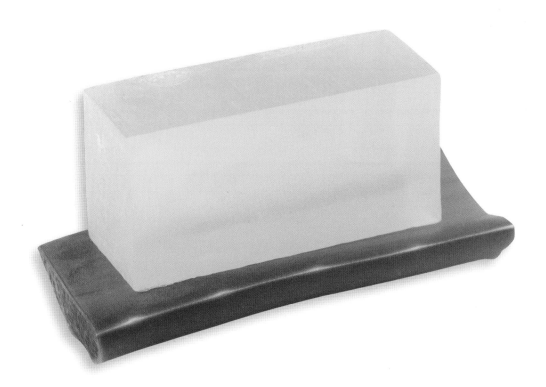

ECHINACEA SOAP

Purple Silk

Echinacea (*Echinacea angustifolia*) is an herb that grows wild in the grasslands of North America, but it can also be grown in your own garden.

It is well known in herbal medicine because it helps the body's immune system quite effectively. The roots and entire plant are taken in powder form, extracts or tinctures, and, to a lesser extent, in infusions or decoctions. Externally, echinacea has a certain antibiotic effect. It acts as a fungicide, bactericide and inhibitor of viral growth.

Native Americans placed echinacea on wounds to prevent them from getting infected and to accelerate the healing process. Settlers to North America learned of the plant's properties from the natives, but in time attributed new qualities to echinacea that had not been demonstrated previously. In fact, settlers used the plant to treat syphilis and gonorrhea.

After some years, people stopped having faith in echinacea. In the second half of the 20th century, however, its true properties were rediscovered, including its action as a barrier plant against fungi, viruses and bacteria, both on the skin and in the immune system. They say that a person who takes echinacea daily will be free of colds and flu throughout the year.

It has been shown that taking echinacea improves the elimination of toxins, damaged cells and other elements that harm the body. Echinacea is also responsible for helping regenerate tissue and reduce scars.

Echinacea Soap

7.5 oz	mineral water	213 g
3 oz	lye (caustic soda)	85 g
1.5 lbs	extra virgin olive oil	682 g
0.35 oz	beeswax	10 g
	A handful of echinacea flower petals (optional)	
0.07 oz	echinacea essential oil	2 g

1. Wearing gloves and goggles, pour mineral water into a large saucepan. Add lye slowly, stirring gently until it is dissolved.

2. Using a thermometer, monitor the temperature of the lye mixture until it is between 120°F and 140°F (49°C and 60°C).

3. Meanwhile, in a separate saucepan, heat olive oil to between 120°F and 140°F (49°C and 60°C), stirring in beeswax slowly.

4. Remove olive oil mixture from heat. Add lye mixture to olive oil mixture, stirring slowly and trying not to splash.

5. Stir occasionally, every 15 minutes or so, until the mixture thickens and congeals. (It will have a texture similar to that of light mayonnaise.)

6. Stir in echinacea petals (if using) and essential oil. Stir for 1 minute with a spoon (or with a whisk, taking care not to create any foam).

7. Pour into a greased or paper-lined soap mold. Gently tap mold to remove any air bubbles.

8. Cover with a blanket or towel and let stand for 2 days. Uncover and let stand for an additional day if the mold is very large.

9. Turn soap out of mold. Wait another day, then cut into bars as desired.

10. Dry bars for 1 month, turning occasionally to ensure they are drying uniformly.

Echinacea Soap's Action on the Skin

- Echinacea can play a major role as an antiseptic for treating wounds, acne, boils, burns or any other type of external attack on the skin.

- In addition to healing wounds, this soap has insecticidal properties attributed to it. In other words, if you wash yourself with it, mosquitoes will stay away.

- Echinacea promotes tissue regeneration and scar formation at the site of an injury. There have been rare cases of allergies with severe itching reported, so test the soap on a small area first.

ROSE HIP SOAP

The Essence of Youth

The sweetbrier rose (*Rosa eglanteria*) belongs to the Rosaceae family. It is said to have originated in Europe, but it colonized the New World many years ago.

Since this plant thrives in temperate climates, it grows especially well in the Andes Mountains in Chile and in Patagonia in Argentina, where the Mapuche people use the oil extracted from its seeds (inside the rose hips, or the fruits of the plant) to ward off wrinkles caused by the cold. The shrub has slender, spine-covered branches, which fill with white and pink flowers, thus adding a bit of cheer to the Patagonian wilderness.

In North America, the oil is also used to remove stretch marks that appear on the belly after pregnancy. Some experts also call the sweetbrier rose "the flower of youth."

Rose hip seed oil is rich in polyunsaturated, linoleic, oleic and linolenic essential fatty acids, which contribute to skin regeneration. It is increasingly being included in the composition of cosmetic products, especially those that help promote scar healing for people who have undergone surgery.

Rose Hip Soap

Wrinkles, spots, stretch marks and scars disappear with this combination of ingredients. This soap also reduces blemishes and moisturizes the skin.

Fun Facts

Sweetbrier roses are cultivated in the United Kingdom, but only grow wild in Argentina and Chile, in the foothills of the Andes, where the oil from the seeds is extracted for cosmetic purposes.

The aroma of the sweetbrier rose is a powerful stimulant.

Note: Exact measurements are crucial in soap making. Turn to page 21 for how-tos.

7.5 oz	mineral water	213 g
3 oz	lye (caustic soda)	85 g
1.5 lbs	extra virgin olive oil	682 g
0.35 oz	beeswax	10 g
1 tbsp	wild rose petals	15 mL
0.7 oz	rose hip seed oil	20 g

1. Wearing gloves and goggles, pour mineral water into a large saucepan. Add lye slowly, stirring gently until it is dissolved.

2. Using a thermometer, monitor the temperature of the lye mixture until it is between 120°F and 140°F (49°C and 60°C).

3. Meanwhile, in a separate saucepan, heat olive oil to between 120°F and 140°F (49°C and 60°C), stirring in beeswax slowly.

4. Remove olive oil mixture from heat. Add lye mixture to olive oil mixture, stirring slowly and trying not to splash.

5. Stir occasionally, every 15 minutes or so, until the mixture thickens and congeals. (It will have a texture similar to that of light mayonnaise.)

6. Stir in rose petals and rose hip seed oil. Stir for 1 minute with a spoon (or with a whisk, taking care not to create any foam).

7. Pour into a greased or paper-lined soap mold. Gently tap mold to remove any air bubbles.

8. Cover with a blanket or towel and let stand for 2 days. Uncover and let stand for an additional day if the mold is very large.

9. Turn soap out of mold. Wait another day, then cut into bars as desired.

10. Dry bars for 1 month, turning occasionally to ensure they are drying uniformly.

Rose Hip Soap's Action on the Skin

❧ Rose hip soap has a distinctive fragrance that appeals to many people. It regenerates and nourishes the skin, fighting the appearance of wrinkles and spots. This effect will be reinforced if rose hip seed oil is applied to the body after washing.

❧ The healing properties of rose hips were discovered after a scientific study conducted in Chile demonstrated that the oil's continued use effectively reduced scars and wrinkles and rejuvenated the skin.

❧ An excellent antiseptic, rose hip soap can be used to cleanse the skin after a simple operation or to wash burns.

Resources

Associations

Canadian Association of Professional Soap & Cosmetic Crafters

www.canadianprofessionalsoap
makers.com

*Association of professional
craftspeople specializing in artisanal
soaps and personal care products.*

The European Directory of Soap and Cosmetic Makers

146 Glasgow Rd.
Longcroft, Stirlingshire
FK4 1QL, U.K.
www.soapmakers.eu

*Europe's largest directory of artisans
specializing in handmade soaps,
candles, cosmetics and personal
care products.*

Handcrafted Soap and Cosmetic Guild

178 Elm St.
Saratoga Springs, NY 12866, U.S.A.
www.soapguild.org

*International nonprofit trade
association promoting the benefits
of handcrafted soap and cosmetics.*

Supplies

Aussie Soap Supplies

P.O. Box 165
Palmyra, WA 6957, Australia
www.aussiesoapsupplies.com.au

*Base and essential oils, cocoa butter,
beeswax, lye, additives and molds.*

Bramble Berry Soap Making Supplies

2138 Humboldt St.
Bellingham, WA 98225, U.S.A.
www.brambleberry.com

*Base and essential oils, cocoa butter,
beeswax, lye, additives, tools and molds.*

Canwax Candle & Soap Supplies

114 Lindgren Rd. W.
Huntsville, ON P1H 1Y2, Canada
www.canwax.com

*Base and essential oils, cocoa butter,
lye and tools.*

Elk Mountain Herbs

214 Ord St.
Laramie, WY 82070, U.S.A.
www.elkmountainherbs.com

*Tinctures, bulk herbs, teas and
ceremonial herbs.*

From Nature with Love

341 Christian St.
Oxford, CT 06478, U.S.A.
www.fromnaturewithlove.com
Base and essential oils, cocoa butter,
beeswax, Dead Sea salt, clays
and additives.

Gracefruit Limited

146 Glasgow Rd.
Longcroft, Stirlingshire
FK4 1QL, U.K.
www.gracefruit.com
Base and essential oils, cocoa butter,
beeswax, exfoliants, clays, salts
and additives.

Healing Spirits Herb Farm

61247 Route 415
Avoca, NY 14809, U.S.A.
www.healingspiritsherbfarm.com
Bulk herbs, essential oils and
herb extracts.

Horizon Herbs

P.O Box 69
William, OR 97544, U.S.A.
www.horizonherbs.com
Bulk herbs, extracts, seeds and plants.

Mountain Rose Herbs

P.O. Box 50220
Eugene, OR 97405, U.S.A.
www.mountainroseherbs.com
Bulk herbs, teas, cocoa butter,
beeswax, and base and essential oils.

New Directions Aromatics

6781 Columbus Rd.
Mississauga, ON L5T 2G9, Canada
www.newdirectionsaromatics.ca
Base and essential oils, cocoa butter,
beeswax, tools and molds.

Oregon Trail Soapers Supply

P. O. Box 1456
Rogue River, OR 97537, U.S.A.
www.oregontrailsoaps.com
Base and essential oils, cocoa butter,
beeswax, clays, additives and molds.

Richters

357 Hwy 47
Goodwood, ON L0C 1A0, Canada
www.richters.com
Bulk herbs, essential oils, seeds
and plants.

Saffire Blue

1444 Bell Mill Rd.
Tillsonburg, ON N4G 4G9, Canada
www.saffireblue.ca
Base and essential oils, cocoa butter,
beeswax, lye, Dead Sea and other
salts, additives, molds and stamps.

Sage Woman Herbs

108 East Cheyenne Rd.
Colorado Springs, CO 80906, U.S.A.
www.sagewomanherbs.com
Bulk herbs, capsules, essential oils,
tinctures and teas.

Soap Basics

23 Southbrook Rd.
Melksham, Wiltshire
SN12 8DS, U.K.
www.soapbasics.com
Base and essential oils, cocoa butter, beeswax, additives and molds.

The Soap Kitchen

Unit 8, Caddsdown Industrial Park
Clovelly Rd.
Bideford, Devon, EX39 3DX, U.K.
www.thesoapkitchen.co.uk
Base oils, cocoa butter, beeswax, plant extracts, additives and molds.

Soapmakers Store

Unit 3, Quatro Park
Blakelands Industrial Estate
Tanners Drive
Milton Keynes MK14 5FJ, U.K.
http://soapmakers-store.com
Cocoa butter, beeswax, additives and molds.

Voyageur Soap & Candle Company, Ltd.

#14-19257 Enterprise Way
Surrey, BC V3S 6J8, Canada
www.voyageursoapandcandle.com
Base and essential oils, cocoa butter, beeswax, lye, molds and tools.

Library and Archives Canada Cataloguing in Publication

Gómez, Mar (María del Mar)
[Jabones naturales para hacer en casa. English]
    The best natural homemade soaps : 40 recipes for moisturizing olive oil-based soaps / Mar Gómez.

Includes index.
Translation of: Jabones naturales para hacer en casa.
ISBN 978-0-7788-0490-1 (pbk.)

    1. Soap. 2. Essences and essential oils. I. Title.

TP991.G66 2014   668'.12   C2014-903336-2

Index